ESSENTIAL
VOLKSWAGEN
KARMANN-GHIA

ESSENTIAL
VOLKSWAGEN
KARMANN-GHIA

THE CARS AND THEIR STORY
1955-74

L A U R E N C E   M E R E D I T H

Published 1994 by Bay View Books Ltd
The Red House, 25–26 Bridgeland Street,
Bideford, Devon EX39 2PZ

Reprinted 1996

© Copyright 1994 by Bay View Books Ltd
Edited by Mark Hughes
Designed by Peter Laws
Computer make-up by Chris Fayers

ISBN 1 870979 52 4
Printed in Hong Kong

CONTENTS

BIRTH OF THE KARMANN-GHIA

Wilhelm Karmann founded his company in 1874 in order to build horse-drawn coaches. This activity was relatively short-lived because, just 11 years later, Karl Benz revealed the world's first internal combustion engined car, a motor tricycle, which by the end of the 19th century would radically alter the working practices of Europe's coachbuilders.

Karmann was typical, and by 1902 his Osnabrück factory was busy making motor car bodies for Dürkopp. Within a short time, the company was working for other motor manufacturers, including Hansa-Lloyd and Adler, both now defunct. Karmann was generally successful, but like so many other manufacturing companies, it was to suffer from the economic depression of the late 1920s and early 1930s. But thanks to continuing contracts with Adler and others it managed to remain afloat.

Built in secrecy during 1953, the shapely prototype lacked fresh air intakes in the front panel and the indicators were inset, but by and large the production coupés faithfully followed the original car. The prototype now has non-original one-piece bumpers.

After World War II, Karmann's Osnabrück factory lay in tatters. Rebuilding it was a slow process, so the firm was unable to return to its former coachbuilding business until 1949. Karmann had previously collaborated with several motor manufacturers, but after the appointment of Heinz Nordhoff as Volkswagen's chief executive in January 1948, the immediate future of the Osnabrück concern lay firmly at the feet of the Wolfsburg giant.

Having been given approval by Nordhoff, Karmann constructed several prototypes of a new Beetle cabriolet during the late 1940s and, after an

Shapely Ghia badge and Karmann script, mounted on the front wing, are unique to the prototype.

Whether it was designed by Virgil Exner in the USA or by Mario Boano in Italy – and there is some doubt – the Karmann's styling looks far from dated today.

intensive test and development programme, put the car into full-scale production in 1949. Such was the demand for the Beetle cabriolet that Karmann had completed its 1000th car by the spring of 1950 and more than 330,000 by the time production ended in January 1980.

Despite the success of the cabriolet, Wilhelm Karmann's ambition was to build a car of his own, *à la* Porsche, but unfortunately he died in 1951 and never saw his dream come to fruition. However, as early as 1950 his company had started negotiations with Volkswagen for a joint venture to produce a sports car.

The idea was to create a two-seater convertible based on a Beetle platform chassis, and Dr Wilhelm Karmann, son of the company's founder, had several discussions to that end with Dr Feuereisen, Volkswagen's vice president, and Ludwig Boehner, Volkswagen's product development director. The Beetle chassis and running gear made an obvious choice because reliability and durability were already legendary, even if engine performance was lacking. But more of that later.

Karmann built scale models based on its own designs, but none found favour with the upper

7

It is interesting to compare the similarities between the prototype, now proudly displayed in Karmann's museum in Osnabrück, and the last production versions made in 1974.

echelons of the Wolfsburg management team. A low-slung sporting car just did not look right on the narrow Beetle platform, and there was another problem to overcome.

Nordhoff was a careful, conservative man who, having been charged with the considerable task of making a success of the Beetle, was not about to be distracted by the ideals of 'outsiders' who wanted to press ahead with an expensive coachbuilt sports car at a time when West Germany was in the process of rebuilding its still fragile economy. Nordhoff was reluctant to take the risk of launching new models, firmly believing that the way forward for Volkswagen was the continual refinement of the Beetle.

During the late 1940s, Nordhoff had agreed to the production of the Transporter (officially launched in 1950), to the Karmann-built Beetle cabriolet and the short-lived Hebmüller two-seater cabriolet. Beyond

these, he would not go, for the time being at least. Persisting with its idea for a sporting Volkswagen throughout 1950, 1951 and 1952, but making little headway at Wolfsburg, Karmann turned its attention instead to Carrozzeria Ghia in Turin, and more particularly to commercial director Luigi Segre.

Dr Karmann had often met Segre at motor shows, and early in 1953 spoke to him about the possibility of a Beetle-based sports car. Karmann went further and asked Segre to build a prototype in Turin with a view to convincing Volkswagen of the project's merits at a later date. Segre was obviously impressed with Karmann's idea, because a short time later, in March, he visited Volkswagen's Paris-based French importer, Charles Ladouche, in order to acquire a Beetle saloon as a basis for the project.

For obvious reasons, Volkswagen was not told of this 'clandestine' operation, but it is a little strange that even Dr Karmann was apparently unaware of Segre's visit to Paris and his acquisition of the new Beetle. Once back in Turin with his prize, Segre and his team began work on the new prototype, but here the story of what would eventually become the Karmann-Ghia coupé takes on something of a twist.

From the events that led up to Segre's meeting with Dr Karmann and his subsequent visit to Ladouche in Paris, it is not unlikely that the timeless styling of what many came to regard as Volkswagen's most beautiful motor car was actually drawn not in Italy, but in America, by Virgil Exner. This talented man, who was head of Pontiac's design studio by the age of 25, joined Raymond Loewy's studio in 1939 and worked as the chief stylist there for Studebaker's various new projects.

Later he joined Chrysler under the company's chief stylist, Henry King, where his influence in shaping that company's products quickly became obvious. During his time with Chrysler, Exner was also granted permission to design advanced prototype vehicles for show purposes, but with a view to incorporating his distinctive styling features into production cars of the future. Exner's powerful enthusiasm for such projects understandably led him to become a little frustrated with the time it took for his drawings to be turned into working motor cars.

As a result of a visit by Luigi Segre to Chrysler in 1951, Exner found another welcome outlet for his design work. On that occasion, Segre had brought with him a Ghia design for a car based on a Plymouth chassis, the XX500, which had been commissioned by Chrysler's vice president, C.B. Thomas. Exner was shown the design and quickly formed the opinion that Ghia would be able to turn his designs into reality in its Turin workshops.

Segre was awarded a contract there and then to build bodies for Chryslers drawn by Virgil Exner, beginning with the K-310, a two-seater with a distinctive low swage line that ran along the bottom of the doors and curved upwards over the rear wings. A further Exner design, the Coupe d'Elegance, resembled the Karmann-Ghia coupé even more closely in some respects, and was built in Ghia's workshops for Chrysler early in 1953 at roughly the same time that Ghia was working on the Karmann prototype. Apart from providing Ghia with scale drawings from which to build the Coupe d'Elegance, Chrysler also supplied a plaster model. When the Karmann coupé was eventually revealed, Exner claimed that it was a scaled-down version of his original design.

Exner's claim is highly debateable, because it is just as likely that the Karmann-Ghia was designed as early as 1950 by Mario Boano. Having worked with Farina early in his career, Boano set up his own design firm in the mid-1930s. He was so successful that he was

The prototype was fitted with sumptuous leather seats, but the steering wheel, speedometer, door handles and switchgear were all from Wolfsburg.

This beautifully stylised illustration is typical of early Karmann-Ghia publicity.

able to buy the Ghia concern in 1948, having entered into a partnership agreement two years previously. Boano was responsible for several interesting car designs in the post-war period, including the Alfa Romeo 6C 2500S and Lancia Aurelia, both of which have some similarities with the body styling of the later Karmann-Ghia.

By 1950, the idea of using a Beetle platform chassis as the basis for a glamorous sports car was not new. After all, Porsche had built its Type 64, an attractive alloy-bodied coupé intended for the Berlin-Rome road race in 1939, so it is not inconceivable that this car gave Boano inspiration for a similar idea. Mario Boano's claim is at least plausible, and if he did set down the designs for what was to become the Karmann-Ghia as early as 1950, the fact that the prototype was not built for another three years can be explained by Volkswagen's refusal to make available a spare chassis on which to construct it.

The truth as to who really designed the Karmann-Ghia will probably never be known. It is said that great minds think alike and perhaps both Exner and Boano came up with similar designs at roughly the same time. Certainly both men influenced the final design in their own way, for whatever Exner's claim about the rear end and side treatment of the Ghia's bodywork, there is little doubt that Boano was responsible for the shapely front.

The Karmann-Ghia prototype was built in some secrecy in just a few months during 1953, and was

shown in early autumn to Dr Karmann in Paris, not in Turin as one might expect. It could be that if Karmann had visited the Turin workshops, he would have seen the Exner-designed Coupe d'Elegance. On the other hand, Segre had acquired the Beetle that was to form the basis of the Karmann-Ghia from Ladouche in Paris, so the French capital was perhaps not such an obscure choice for revealing the prototype to Dr Karmann. The car's existence came as a complete surprise to him, in particular when he discovered that it was a beautifully proportioned coupé and not a convertible as he had originally envisaged.

From the outset, it was inevitable that the new car could not be put into production without modifications to the Beetle's platform chassis. In standard form, the floorpans either side of the central backbone were too narrow to accommodate the 'full-width' body, so Karmann's design engineers drew up plans to widen them.

It was at this stage that Heinz Nordhoff was invited to look at the prototype. Eventually he reached a double-edged conclusion, pronouncing it very beautiful on the one hand and much too expensive to put into production on the other. After listening to Dr Karmann's proposals, though, Nordhoff had second thoughts. The car was to be built and assembled by Karmann on Beetle rolling chassis supplied by Wolfsburg, and sold through the Volkswagen dealer network alongside the Beetle cabriolet, the Beetle saloon and the Transporter. On that basis, the new car

**Early Karmann sales
literature is now rare,
expensive and highly
regarded in the
automotive art world.**

would be economically viable, and Nordhoff gave it his blessing.

A small number of cars were built for test purposes, and heavily disguised as they were to be driven on public roads. Apart from having to widen the floorpans by 80mm on each side, Karmann's engineers encountered relatively few difficulties in adapting the Beetle chassis to fit the new body. The steering column had to be tilted downwards and the gear lever had to be shortened because of the low seating position, but throughout 1954 the car was slowly readied for production. In fact Karmann's biggest problem at that time was that, as a traditional coachbuilding company, it had no large presses and the result was that the steel bodies had to be largely assembled by hand on purpose-built jigs. In the initial stages, this was a labour intensive operation. The nose of the car alone was assembled using no fewer than five separate panels welded together, the joins between each being expertly smoothed out with lead. And unlike the Beetle, the Karmann's front and rear wings were welded to the shell rather than being bolted.

An early Karmann publicity shot shows the handsome body to good effect, but the hub cap emblems give the game away about the car's true nature.

Extremely complex in construction, the Karmann's bodyshell consists of dozens of small panels, the largest of which comprise the roof, front and rear wings, doors, bonnet and engine lid. Under the skin, there are separate panels for the spare wheel well, the apron that forms the floor of the luggage bay, bulkhead, dashboard and inner wings. An equally bewildering number of panels are used for the rear of the car, the largest forming the rear luggage bay and engine 'firewall'. The inner wings are comparatively small and there are transverse strengthening panels fitted in front of the floor of the luggage bay. There is a separate rear bulkhead below the window and a separate panel for the rear valance. After being welded, the entire bodyshell was bolted to the Volkswagen platform chassis, with a rubberised belt placed between the two to create an air-tight seal.

Not surprisingly, Karmann followed the design of the Ghia-built prototype very closely when it came to building the production cars. There were some small external differences: air intake vents were added to the nose; the bumpers, originally divided, became single blades; and the front indicators were positioned directly below the headlamps instead of being inset on the front panel. But generally Karmann was confident that the stunning beauty of the styling had been exactly right first time.

The car's press launch was originally intended for 27 August 1955, but the date had to be brought forward because, incredibly, the small Karmann factory did not have enough space to store the cars through the summer months. Instead 14 July was chosen and the venue was the Kasino Hotel in Westfalen, close to Osnabrück. Officially, the car had no name, so Dr Karmann simply put his own company's name in front of Ghia in recognition of the Italian company's important role in the project, and that was that.

Needless to say, press reaction was most favourable. Although fewer than 40 cars were sent out to dealers' showrooms during August, daily production increased considerably after the official public launch at the Frankfurt Motor Show in September. By the end of December the company had produced 500 cars. This rose to some 10,000 before the end of the following year, and all the time Karmann was keeping up with increasing demand for the Beetle cabriolet which was built alongside the coupé on the same assembly lines.

It had taken five years from the time that the Karmann project was first mooted to the coupé's public launch. The intense and now legendary behind-the-scenes wrangling during those years was the stuff of successful political thriller writers. Through all the difficulties, though, common sense won the day for the Karmann-Ghia. It was certainly an expensive motor car, but by the late 1950s society had become affluent once again and Karmann, like Porsche and so many others, capitalised on a growing market for beautifully made and styled sporting cars.

THE RANGE IN BRIEF

The idea of the Karmann-Ghia was to offer customers the look and feel of a high quality hand-built sports car without the normal running costs. In many respects it was unique. No other manufacturer had a direct rival in its range during the mid-1950s, and although the concept of utilising a custom-built body to clothe a 'cooking' chassis and mechanicals would eventually catch on at Renault (with the Floride) and Volvo (the P1800), the Karmann-Ghia created a market of its own.

Initially, the Type 1 coupé (designated 143 in Volkswagen's complex numbering system) was available only with left-hand drive, and production was planned for 50 cars per day. The streamlined bodywork included several advanced features more normally associated with cars costing at least twice as much as the DM7500 asked for the Ghia. There were elegant, pillarless doors, hinged at the front and a full metre wide to allow easy access to the cabin. The

The coupé was an instant success in every market in which it was sold. Distinctive European styling particularly appealed to the Americans, who were largely responsible for the Karmann-Ghia's long production run of nearly 19 years.

window glass curved gently inward at the top, rather than being flat. In keeping with the times, chromium plating was used extensively for the exterior trim.

Without doubt, this stunning coupé had style. And whereas no-one remained indifferent to the Beetle, the Karmann-built coupé boasted universal appeal. Every known cliché has been used to describe the Karmann-Ghia, but few have put the styling into perspective as well as the English journalist, John Bolster, writing in *Autosport*: 'This is not only a very lovely car, but it is a new artistic conception. For years, it has been conventional to worship the cult of the long bonnet, and some hideous vehicles have been

applauded in consequence. It all stems from antique times, when the car with a long nose was assumed to have a powerful engine, and therefore to be excitingly fast. This has been the reason for victories in concours d'elegance of ill-proportioned devices, in which the box containing the engine has occupied most of the chassis and the wealthy proprietor and his mink-clad companion have been banished to the infernal regions near the back axle.'

The car's appearance in the mid-1950s created something of a sensation, the well-proportioned lines of its graceful body giving little indication of the position of the engine hung out in the tail or the mundane nature of the Beetle mechanicals under the hand-crafted skin.

Production cars differed from the prototype externally in having two intake slots in the nose for fresh air ventilation in the cabin, and for decoration these each received two horizontal chromed slats. Instead of being cut transversely, the intake louvres on the engine lid became vertical in four banks. In Beetle fashion, the front bonnet catch was released by a

It was no surprise when Karmann, a long-established coachbuilder, launched a convertible version in August 1957.

cable-operated pull-knob under the left-hand side of the dashboard, but the Karmann differed from the Beetle in that the engine lid was also operated in the same way, by a pull-knob located near the sill on the driver's side.

Mechanically, the Karmann-Ghia was pure Beetle. In 1954, Wolfsburg uprated the original 1131cc 25bhp engine by increasing its size to 1192cc and power output to 30bhp. When the Karmann coupé was launched in 1955 the 30bhp engine was fitted and remained in place until the Beetle's revised 1192cc unit with 34bhp became available in 1960. The only difference between Beetle and Karmann-Ghia applications was the air-cleaner. Because the body of the coupé was so much lower, the traditional Beetle oil bath air-cleaner was replaced by the one fitted to the Volkswagen Transporter, and positioned on the left-hand side of the Karmann-Ghia's engine bay. This

First shown to the public at the Frankfurt Motor Show in 1961, the Type 3 Karmann-Ghia was intended as a successor to the then six-year-old Type 1, but unusual styling and a high price tag ensured that it was not a success.

slight modification, in turn, led to a change in the Solex carburettor's main jet air bleed from 195 to 180. And because there was so much space in the engine bay, the six-volt battery, which in the Beetle was sited under the rear seat on the right-hand side, was located in the Karmann-Ghia's engine compartment on the right-hand side.

Virtually all of the mechanical revisions made to the Beetle at Wolfsburg were carried through to the Karmann-Ghia at the beginning of each new model year in August, which is why the four-speed gearbox had to soldier on without synchromesh on bottom gear until 1960. The Karmann-Ghia's chassis differed slightly from the Beetle's, but only in floorpan width and some minute details.

The Beetle's Porsche-designed torsion bar springing was retained front and rear. Curiously, the Karmann-Ghia was fitted with a 12mm front anti-roll bar from the start whereas the Beetle did not acquire one until 1960. The anti-roll bar had a dramatic effect on the car's roadholding compared with a Beetle. Writing in *Autosport* and making a general comment about the Karmann-Ghia's road manners, John Bolster said: 'The improvement in riding and handling has to be experienced to be believed. Gone altogether is the typical VW oversteer, and one can drive fast on wet roads without the uneasy feeling that the tail is about to wag the dog. Gone too is that choppy up and down

movement at low speeds on bumpy lanes. The weight distribution has obviously been improved and the centre of gravity has been lowered.'

The coupé was an instant success in every market in which it was sold, and gave Karmann the inspiration and impetus to build a convertible version. Production began on 1 August 1957, but the car was not shown to the public until the Frankfurt Motor Show the following month. Once again, the reaction from the press and public alike was very positive even though the DM8250 purchase price was DM750 more than the price of the coupé.

Karmann had long been keen on a production two-seater convertible and had constructed a prototype back in 1954. This old-established coachbuilding company knew all about 'rag-top' construction, so Karmann's engineers had no need to seek advice from Ghia in Turin.

Without the roof, the bodyshell's torsional stiffness naturally disappeared, so Karmann concentrated its efforts on strengthening the body and chassis accordingly. Additional reinforcing metal resulted in a weight penalty and a decrease in the car's overall performance, but for those who wanted to experience the joys of wind-in-the-hair motoring, Volkswagen style, it was a small price to pay.

Introduced for the 1967 model year, the 1500 version is possibly the most desirable Karmann-Ghia, particularly as a 'rag top', because it combined the reliability of the 1200 with the performance of the later 1600.

The car was just as aesthetically pleasing with the canvas hood up or down, and in one way held a clear advantage over the Beetle cabriolet. Being a full four-seater, the Beetle had a necessarily large hood which, when folded down, formed a cumbersome structure that adversely affected the engine's cooling system at high speeds. The two-seater Karmann-Ghia's hood was inherently smaller and, in folding down more compactly, had little effect on the flow of air to the engine lid's intake louvres.

The left-hand drive convertible was numbered 141 by Volkswagen, while right-hand drive versions of the convertible and coupé, which were both available from 1959, became 142 and 144 respectively.

By the late 1950s the entire Volkswagen range, which consisted of the Beetle, the Transporter and the Karmann-Ghia, was selling exceptionally well all over the world, but particularly in North America. Sales went from strength to strength and Nordhoff interpreted the annual balance sheets to mean that Volkswagen's customers wanted more, much more, of the same. While the rest of the world's manufacturers brought out one new model after another, Volkswagen merely updated existing products.

Criticism of Nordhoff's policy by influential journalists on both sides of the Atlantic made little difference to this autocrat. Some even thought – and foolishly committed to print – that in launching the Karmann-Ghia Volkswagen had given a tantalising hint of the shape of things to come. After all, so many experts had predicted that the days of the age-old Beetle, with its noisy air-cooled engine, pre-war chassis and cramped interior, were numbered, and even Nordhoff occasionally had second thoughts.

A replacement for the Beetle did seem inevitable at some stage, and Porsche had an interesting three-box saloon in the pipeline, the Type 726, which was developed for Volkswagen in 1958. With its conventional saloon styling, the Type 3 Volkswagen also developed by Porsche was eventually launched to the public in 1961, but instead of replacing the Beetle, which was selling far too well to be dropped, it was produced alongside it. The Type 3 had a newly-designed, air-cooled 1500 engine mounted in the rear, a larger platform chassis with a central backbone tunnel, and torsion bar suspension front and rear, but there the resemblance to the Beetle ended.

The 1500 engine was developed throughout 1958 and 1959. It differed from the normal Beetle 1200 unit in having its cooling fan mounted on the nose of the crankshaft instead of in an upright position above the engine. The result was a much more compact and 'flatter' power unit which gave the Type 3 saloon an additional luggage space in the tail and also allowed an estate 'Variant' version to be built. Nordhoff also proposed convertible saloon, sporting coupé and sports

After just seven years, production of the Type 3 Karmann came to an end to make way for the VW-Porsche 914, a car with equally unusual styling and a similarly short production life.

convertible versions of the Type 3, all three of which were to be built by Karmann.

Carrozzeria Ghia had been working on designs for the 1500 versions of a coupé since 1958, and the Italian company's director of styling, Sergio Sartorelli, had completed three design proposals just three days after Ghia was awarded the contract by Volkswagen. One of these three designs was chosen and Sartorelli had a working prototype completed by the end of 1959. Some changes had been made to it by the time it was unveiled at the Frankfurt Show in September 1961, but by and large it remained the same.

Officially known as the Type 34 Karmann-Ghia (but commonly referred to as the Type 3 Karmann-Ghia), it had controversial styling for the time. Where the Type 1 was curvaceous and pretty, the new car looked aggressive and purposeful. The rear end was angular and most attractive, but the frontal treatment was less happy and the sharply-cut 'eyebrows' above the quad-headlamp layout did not find favour in all quarters. Typically, no motoring journalists of the time were brave enough to come clean and say that the car was ugly. Hansjorg Bendel commented in *Road & Track*: 'Beautiful or not, giving the car the "different look" was a compulsory design target which – not many will doubt this – was accomplished.'

The Type 34 was put into production at the Karmann factory in March 1962 and built alongside the Type 1 coupé and convertible, but proposals for producing convertible versions of the Type 34 and the Type 3 four-seater were shelved.

Unlike the Type 1 Karmann-Ghia, the Type 3 was not a success. As the flagship of the range, it should have been. It was the only Volkswagen with integral fog lights and an electrically-operated sunroof. Mechanically, it followed the Type 3 saloon and variant range. The 45bhp 1493cc engine pushed up top speed to nearly 80mph and the benchmark 0-60mph figure could be achieved from rest in under 20sec, but it cost almost as much to buy as a Porsche 356 and, for that reason, was never officially exported to the USA.

The engine capacity was increased to 1584cc for 1966 and the top speed increased accordingly to 94mph. A fully automatic gearbox was introduced as an option for 1967, whereas the Type 1 had the option of the semi-automatic 'box as fitted to the Beetle. The car was dropped from the range in July 1969 to make way for the VW-Porsche 914. Just 42,498 were produced, of which 30,000 were sold in Germany and the rest were exported to Britain, Australia, New Zealand, Canada and Europe.

Meanwhile, the Type 1 soldiered on. In keeping with the development of the Beetle, the original Karmann-Ghia in both coupé and convertible guises was treated to the 40bhp 1285cc engine for the 1966

Despite undergoing many thousands of detail modifications before production ended in 1974, the Type 1 remained largely unaltered in concept and shape.

model year and the 44bhp 1493cc unit the following year. The 50bhp 1584cc engine from the 1302S Beetle was fitted in 1970 and production for Germany ended in 1973. The last chassis for the European market were made on 21 December and had chassis numbers 144 2376 366 (Type 141 convertible) and 144 2376 681 (Type 143 coupé). Production continued specifically for the American market for a further six months, and finally ended on 21 June 1974 with chassis numbers 144 2780 500 (Type 143) and 144 2780 502 (Type 141). Thereafter, the Osnabrück factory was turned over to production of the Scirocco.

That the Type 1 Karmann-Ghia survived for so long is astonishing. For other manufacturers in the Western world, the key to marketing success was the launch of new models, yet Volkswagen and Karmann plodded on with the same basic cars. They were certainly modified and updated at the beginning of each new model year, but, in essence, the cars remained unchanged.

Demand for the coupé certainly declined in the last two or three years of its life, but at that time there was nothing to replace it. Throughout the late 1950s and early 1960s, Volkswagen's management team were aware that a successor to the Beetle would have to be found. The Type 3 saloon and Karmann-Ghia coupé were both launched in 1961 and were intended to replace the ageing Beetle and the then six-year-old Type 1 Karmann coupé. But the chosen successors were both failures.

In 1968, Volkswagen tried again with the launch of the Type 4 saloon. It too was a failure, as was another intended Beetle successor, the K70, launched in 1970. By this time, new-generation cars from other manufacturers were quieter, more powerful and more economical than anything Volkswagen could provide with its noisy, outdated, air-cooled engines. The car buying public voted, as ever, with their pockets and Volkswagen was caught with its trousers down. The company began to search frantically for new designs which would guarantee its position as Europe's number one motor manufacturer.

A fundamentally different approach was required and Volkswagen's old-established design principles were abandoned. Torsion bar suspension, rear-mounted air-cooled engine, rear-wheel drive and separate body and chassis were dropped once and for all. In their place came MacPherson strut suspension, water-cooled engines, front-wheel drive and unitary construction bodies. After the failure of the K70, which incorporated all of the new design principles, Volkswagen faced the choice of building a car that the public actually wanted or going bankrupt.

Between 1970-74, the latter became a real threat. The Beetle had become a victim of its own success, as had the Karmann-Ghia, and the only hope for Volkswagen was the future of the Golf, launched in 1974. Based on the Golf floorpan and running gear, the pretty Scirocco appeared at the same time. Luckily for Volkswagen and Karmann, both cars were a huge success. It had been a long search for successful Beetle and Karmann-Ghia replacements…

THE TYPE 1 COUPE

At the time of the Volkswagen Karmann-Ghia's launch in 1955, sporting cars were thin on the ground in Germany. In that same year BMW unveiled its 140bhp 3.2-litre V8 507 model, but production was limited to no more than 250 cars over the next five years. Mercedes-Benz offered its exotic 300SL in both coupé and roadster guises, and Porsche had the Beetle-based 356. But all of these cars were extremely expensive.

One of the reasons for this state of affairs has its roots in the mid-1930s. Hitler had given Germany the world's first autobahns and the country's automotive designers, most notably Dr Ferdinand Porsche, began creating cars suited to being driven economically for long periods at high speeds. With its aerodynamically sound body, the Volkswagen Beetle was able to cruise reliably all day and every day at 100kph with nothing

Pre-1959 cars are rare and much sought-after by collectors. From this shot of John Figg's immaculate 1958 car, it is not difficult to appreciate why so many were prepared to forsake the performance of a traditional sports car in favour of the graceful lines of this cleverly designed package from Osnabrück. Note that production cars had fresh-air vents built into the front panel.

more powerful than a 1131cc engine which initially produced a mere 25bhp.

The Karmann-Ghia emerged from the same design philosophy, and its shapely, low-drag body meant that it was even better suited than the Beetle to Germany's growing network of autobahns. Fitted with the 1192cc 30bhp air-cooled flat-four engine introduced into the Beetle in 1954, the Karmann-Ghia had a top speed in

Badging on a 1958 car. Stylish Karmann-Ghia script on the engine lid identifies a collaboration in build and design talent (right), the Karmann badge on the right-hand front wing incorporates Ghia's shield (below) and an attractive V-over-W emblem sits proudly on the nose (below right).

the region of 76mph, which Volkswagen deemed more than adequate for the time. But the Karmann-Ghia was not bought for its performance.

Like the Beetle, the build quality of the Ghia was of the highest order, although corrosion became the car's most potent enemy despite the bodies being dipped in a rust-inhibiting primer. That aside, paint finish and panel fit were second to none and typical of what Volkswagen customers had come to expect. The elegant doors closed with a gentle 'clunk' and British owners soon got used to reprimanding their passengers for slamming them forcefully shut.

The wide cabin was comfortable and spacious, but once installed behind the wheel, the Beetle origins were readily apparent. The two-spoke, ivory-coloured steering wheel with central Wolfsburg crest, the ashtray, the glovebox lid and the speedometer were all taken from Wolfsburg's parts bin. But whereas the

Beetle was fitted with a lone speedometer, the Karmann had a large electric clock installed in the dashboard to the right of the steering column, flanking the speedometer on the left.

Karmann considered that a clock was more useful than the tachometer some of its customers were expecting in a car that, to them, looked more at home on the Mulsanne Straight than gently cruising along the boulevards of a sleepy Parisian suburb. But more useful than a tachometer and a clock would have been a fuel gauge. Instead, there was a reserve fuel tap situated directly above the most forward part of the backbone tunnel on the 'foot' panel. When kicked over by the driver, this tap allowed the last gallon of fuel in the tank to be drawn into the carburettor. This rather ridiculous system was even retained after a separate fuel gauge was introduced in 1957.

The ivory-coloured control knobs for the

The spare wheel and fuel tank intrude significantly into the front luggage space, but this did not bother most owners.

An alloy plate gives information about the Karmann's weights and is fitted to the inside of the right-hand front inner wing.

windscreen wipers and lights were placed to the right of the clock, and the pull-knob for the manual choke was to the left of the speedometer, immediately above the ignition switch. A single stalk on the left-hand side of the steering column operated the indicators. All the controls were well placed, with the exception of the headlamp dip switch which was to the left of the clutch pedal. In view of the fact that six-volt electrics were fitted at this stage, its use was entirely optional. Generously padded, the fully adjustable seats were finished in cloth, as were the interior panels, although leatherette was optional. A radio was also a cost option, but if one was not specified the dashboard was fitted with a removable blanking plate. Behind the

two seats, the generous luggage space could be converted into an occasional rear seat for small children by simply pulling up the cushion forming the 'floor' to create a backrest.

The heating system, which was integrated into the engine's cooling system, relied on air passed over the engine's cylinder barrels, heads and heater boxes built into the exhaust system, and was operated by a rotary knob on the backbone tunnel next to the gear lever – an ingenious arrangement but by no means beyond criticism. The knob operated a cable connected to a control valve and a cooling air outlet flap on each side of the engine. When the knob was rotated clockwise, the cooling air outlet flap was closed off and the heater control valve was opened, allowing hot air to travel through the body sills and into the cabin through outlets at foot level, and on top of the dashboard for windscreen demisting.

The system was flawed in that, if the engine became encrusted in oil and mud, nasty fumes would enter the cabin along with the hot air – which is why Volkswagen modified the system for 1963. Instead of heater boxes, the exhaust pipes were encased in large metal cylinders, or heat exchangers, which ensured that heated fresh air was fed into the cabin instead of hot air that had passed directly over the engine.

Although basic in its fixtures and fittings, the cabin is comfortable, spacious and airy. The seats during the late 1950s were typically of cloth/leatherette and piped with vinyl.

Arguably the best view of the coupé is from the rear, where the only clue to the position of the engine is the row of air intake louvres. This British-registered car is fitted with American-spec bumpers, which have tall overriders and an additional bar above the main blade.

During 1956, the steering wheel was an elegant two-spoke Beetle item (below). This car has a non-standard fuel gauge between the speedometer and the clock. In 1957 the standard Beetle steering wheel was replaced by an ornate Karmann wheel with a semi-circular horn ring (left), and a circular fuel gauge became standard.

Designed by Dr Porsche, the four-cylinder overhead-valve 'boxer' engine was largely unchanged in principle from the prototype cars that had been constructed by Daimler-Benz before the war. Entirely unconventional, the crankcase was made in two halves from light alloy (there being no 'block' in the accepted sense), split vertically and bolted together. The short crankshaft ran in three main bearings with a fourth bearing to support the auxiliary drives. The camshaft was situated below and driven by the crankshaft, and operated pushrods which ran to the cylinder heads immediately below the cast-iron and heavily-finned cylinder barrels.

The crankshaft also drove the dynamo, which was mounted on an alloy pedestal cast into the crankcase, via a belt. Mounted on the end of the dynamo armature shaft, the engine's cooling fan, housed in a steel shroud, drew in air from outside through the intake louvres in the rear engine lid and blew it over the oil cooler, which was mounted on the left-hand side of the crankcase and directly over the engine.

A single Solex 28 PCI carburettor dispensed the fuel/air mixture to the combustion chambers via a long manifold which branched into two pipes immediately below the carb. The manifold ran

transversely across the top of the crankcase and was bolted to the single-port, light-alloy cylinder heads at both ends. Because of the incredibly long distance travelled by the fuel mixture – an inherent drawback of using a single carburettor on a 'boxer' engine – it is common for both the carburettor and the manifold to ice up in cold weather. During the engine's later development, Volkswagen took steps to solve this perennial problem but never eradicated it completely.

Because there is so much room in the Karmann-Ghia's engine bay, access for servicing is much easier than with the Beetle. The engine can be removed

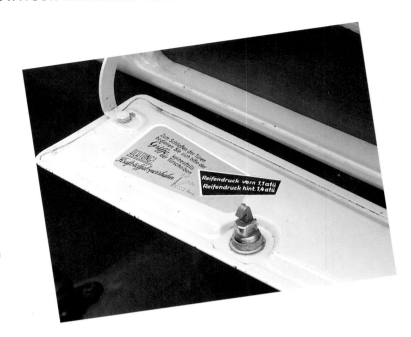

Usefully doubling as a convenient tray for teacups, the glovebox lid also had a label giving information about tyre pressures.

altogether in less than half an hour because it is secured to the gearbox with just four bolts. Compact and dependable, the gearbox and final drive are integrated into one overall unit, and the entire assembly is bolted directly to the sturdy fork at the rear of the chassis.

The light-alloy gearbox casing was split vertically through the middle and bolted together. Porsche-type synchromesh was used for all forward gears except first, and the rear axle assembly – comprising the differential housing, side gears, pinion and shaft, universal joint assemblies and axle shafts – was built into the gearbox. A dry single-plate Fichtel & Sachs clutch was contained within the gearbox bellhousing and operated via a cable which passed through the backbone tunnel.

In keeping with the Beetle and the VW Transporter, the Karmann-Ghia had independent suspension on all four wheels. The front suspension was by parallel trailing arms and torsion bars, the latter housed in two transverse tubes (one on top of the other) bolted directly to the chassis framehead. Torsion bars were also used at the rear and contained within single cylindrical tubes transversely mounted in front of the gearbox. The springs were linked to the swing-axles and hub assemblies with a single trailing arm on each side. Damping was taken care of by double-acting telescopic shock absorbers made by Boge and Hemscheidt.

So tough is the Volkswagen suspension system that the Karmann-Ghia can be driven over rough terrain as quickly as it can on a smooth motorway, and many journalists have been quick to praise its exceptional ride quality. However, the majority were equally quick to condemn the vagaries of the swing-axles. Under exceptionally hard cornering at high speeds, they have a tendency to 'jack' themselves up and cause the wheel under load to 'tuck' itself in. This criticism, which was expounded in virtually every road test ever written, is historically interesting for several reasons.

For motoring enthusiasts brought up on conventional front-engined, rear-wheel drive cars, the rear-engined Volkswagen was something of an enigma. Driving and enjoying a Karmann, or a Beetle, demanded new skills and a different technique at the wheel, which was delightful and rewarding in the extreme once mastered. Much of the criticism aimed at Volkswagen's chassis design came from reactionary journalists who were seemingly determined not to learn the new skills required. Incredibly, their venom was aimed at the swing-axle Mercedes-Benz 300SL as well, but became considerably less toxic after the launch of the Triumph Herald (also fitted with swing-axle rear suspension) in the early 1960s. But more about the Karmann's handling and roadholding later.

The Karmann's steering was by transverse link and unequal length track rods, and the Porsche-designed steering gearbox was by worm and nut. Clamped to the top torsion bar tube, the original type of box was replaced by a much improved drag-free worm and

Early coupés are rare anyway, but a car fitted with a manually-operated Golde sunroof is particularly desirable.

roller unit for the 1962 model year. One can safely ignore *The Autocar*'s April 1961 road test claiming that the coupé had rack and pinion steering...

Entirely conventional, the single-circuit hydraulic braking system had twin-shoe drums all round, with a leading and trailing shoe for each. Mercifully, the cable-operated braking fitted to the standard Beetle was never employed on the Karmann-Ghia. The pressed steel five-stud 15in road wheels were fitted with tubeless crossply tyres. Six-volt electrics were used until 1967, when the entire range, except for the 1200 Beetle, adopted the more satisfactory – and modern – 12-volt system.

Over the years, this initial specification was modified in detail time and time again, mostly by Volkswagen in its enduring quest to achieve the perfect Beetle. The major production changes are discussed next, but, despite the thousands that were made, the shape and concept of the Karmann-Ghia remained unaltered for its 19 years in production.

Production modifications.......................

The most important changes made to the Karmann-Ghia were announced in August at the beginning of each new model year, with minor revisions being made throughout the rest of the year. The first significant modifications were made upon the introduction of the convertible model in September 1957, when a circular fuel gauge was added to the dashboard between the speedometer and the clock (although the reserve fuel tap remained), and the steering wheel, becoming dished, was fitted with a semi-circular horn.

The interior door panels were covered in vinyl rather than cloth and vinyl as previously, and an additional chrome moulding was added to each door panel to make three in all. An armrest was fitted to the right-hand door and there was a larger interior mirror. A more conventional flat accelerator pedal replaced Volkswagen's traditional roller ball. Because the clutch pedal was fitted with a bush bearing, the clutch return spring was made lighter, dropping the pressure to operate the pedal from 6kg to 1kg. The brake shoes were increased in width to 40mm at the front and 30mm at the rear. To reduce engine noise in the cabin, heavy soundproofing material (12mm thick) was fitted to the 'firewall' in the engine bay.

For the 1959 model year, the door hinges were redesigned so that they no longer required lubricating, and at the end of April 1959 (from chassis 2 533 158) the windows and their winding mechanisms were

Because the Karmann's bodywork was so much lower than the Beetle's, the 1192cc 30bhp engine (used in the Beetle between 1954-60) was fitted with the Transporter's air cleaner instead of the ubiquitous oil bath filter arrangement.

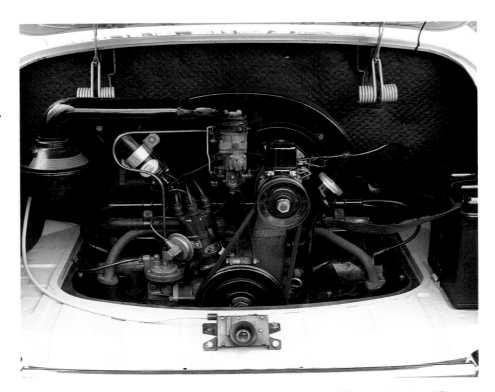

With the rear backrest folded flat, there is generous luggage space in the cabin.

The fold-down rear seat is cramped, but adequate for occasional use by small children. The pull-knob above the sill releases the engine lid.

After August 1959, the front wings were reshaped so that the headlamps were positioned 2in higher, and the air vents on the front panel were enlarged and embellished with three horizontal slats rather than two as previously.

For safety reasons, the rear tail lights were enlarged for the 1960 model year, a sign of increasing traffic even at this stage.

slightly modified. The cost of a new coupé in 1959, incidentally, was DM7500 in Germany, $2318 in the USA and £1166 in Britain.

A minor facelift in August 1959 meant that the headlamps were repositioned 2in higher as a result of modifications to the shape of the front wings, and the air intake slots in the nose were enlarged. At the same time, the latter were embellished with chromed grilles with three horizontal slats rather than two as previously. The rear lights were also enlarged. A steering damper was introduced, windscreen washers were fitted as standard equipment, opening rear side windows were fitted to the coupé and a headlamp flashing function was built into the indicator stalk on the steering column. The reserve fuel tap was dropped. Right-hand drive versions of both the coupé and the convertible were available from the beginning of the 1960 model year and incorporated the same general revisions as their left-hand drive counterparts.

The 1961 model year was something of a watershed as there were sweeping revisions across the entire Volkswagen range, particularly on the mechanical front. As the ultra-reliable 30bhp engine, which had been in service since 1954, was well past its sell-by date, a completely redesigned 34bhp power

unit was installed in its place. Although the 1192cc size remained the same, additional power was obtained by increasing the compression ratio from 6.6:1 to 7.0:1. A stronger crankcase had sturdier studs and bolts, the cylinders were spaced further apart for more efficient cooling, the dynamo pedestal became detachable (instead of being cast into the crankcase) and the cylinder heads were redesigned with wedge-shaped combustion chambers and valves positioned at an angle. A new Solex 28 PICT carburettor replaced the 28 PCI, and included a thermostatically-controlled automatic choke.

The gearbox was also revised to include synchromesh on the bottom ratio, and the alloy casing was cast in one piece instead of being 'split' into two as previously. With its new and larger side bearing

Right-hand drive versions of both the coupé and convertible became available for the British market from August 1959, by which time a Beetle steering wheel was fitted once again.

assemblies, the axle tubes could be removed without the need to dismantle the 'box, a move which made servicing very much easier. Less significant modifications included the fitting of an external mirror on the wing and a smaller 'Karmann Ghia' script on the engine lid.

In its road test of the new car, *Road & Track* was quick to point out that the 11 per cent gain in power made the difference between 'barely adequate performance and that which is satisfactory'. Despite the additional power, the American magazine's road testers could manage a top speed of no more than 75.8mph, a sure indication that the Karmann-Ghia was beginning to put on weight even at this early stage in its life.

For the next four years the Type 1 Karmann-Ghia remained largely unaltered apart from sharing minor modifications aimed at keeping the Beetle up to date. Both Volkswagen and Karmann had been busy during the early part of the 1960s preparing for the launch of the Type 3 range, and development of the existing cars temporarily took second place.

The cabin was better insulated against engine noise for the 1962 model year, and a growing awareness of safety led to seat belt anchorage points being installed, although the belts themselves were optional extras. The VW emblem on the nosecone was also standardised. Previously, cars destined for the American market had a heavy, one-piece chromium-

plated badge whereas those for Europe were fitted with a chromed badge with a blue centre. Upon the introduction of the Type 3 Karmann-Ghia, the emblem became a raised V-over-W logo across the entire Karmann range.

In 1964 the semi-circular horn rim was dropped, the horn being operated instead by elongated thumb buttons recessed into the spokes of the steering wheel. The following year was similarly insignificant for production changes, with some notable exceptions. Before August 1964, the Beetle and the Karmann-Ghia were fitted with a single rotary knob to control the heating system. After that date there were two handles side by side behind the handbrake lever which lay flat when the heater was not in use. The right-hand one, with a red knob, controlled the heat entering the front of the car, while the left-hand one had a white knob and controlled the heating in the rear. In addition, the sun visors could be swivelled through 90 degrees to shade the side windows, and the interior rear view mirror gained a large chromium-plated housing.

By August 1965, both Volkswagen and Karmann were ready to announce more sweeping changes. To the casual observer the 1966 Karmann looked the same, but there were many detail changes which seemed more in the nature of a revolution. The pretty domed hub caps were dropped in favour of flat items and the road wheels were improved by being

This rotary heater knob, a pure Beetle item, was replaced by two lift-up handles in 1964.

After the minor facelift in August 1959, the coupé remained unaltered bodily for many years, the majority of changes taking place under the skin. This car has the flat hub caps introduced for 1966.

ventilated instead of solid, helping to cool the brakes more efficiently.

Because of modifications to the air cleaner, the battery was located on the left-hand side of the engine compartment. The king and link pins on the front suspension were dropped in favour of maintenance-free ball joints, and the external driving mirror, now mounted on a shorter arm instead of the 'swan neck' arm as previously, was repositioned from the front wing to the driver's door. Inside the cabin, the ashtray, finished in chrome or black vinyl, was below the dashboard instead of next to the glovebox. The semi-circular horn ring reappeared, the seats became more supportive and shapely, and the steering wheel became black rather than ivory. But the most welcome changes occurred below the engine lid.

Before this, the heaviest press criticism was rightly centred on the Karmann-Ghia's performance. For a car whose styling looked more at home in Milan, the performance from the 1200 34bhp engine was severely lacking. Volkswagen went part way to silencing dissent by introducing a new 1300 engine, achieved by

utilising the crankshaft from the Type 3 1500 model to lengthen the stroke from 64mm to 69mm and give an overall capacity of 1285cc. The compression ratio was raised from 7:1 to 7.3:1. There was also a larger carburettor, the Solex 30 PICT.

The engine's maximum 40bhp, a 17½ per cent increase over the 34bhp unit, was produced at 4000rpm. By comparison with the 1200, the new 1300 felt lively, with improved acceleration, but a top speed of only 78mph still meant that the car lagged well behind its competitors. A VW 1300 badge on the engine lid distinguished this slightly livelier Karmann-Ghia from the previous 1200 model.

Surprisingly, the 1300 lasted in production only for one model year – there still was not enough power. So, for 1967, Volkswagen introduced its all-time classic: the new 1500. Producing a maximum 44bhp at 4000rpm, the 1493cc unit retained the same stroke as the 1300, but the bore increased from 77mm to 83mm and the compression ratio rose to 7.5:1. In effect, it was the same engine that had seen service in the Type 3 except that the cooling fan was mounted vertically

Distinguished by the additional badge on the engine lid, this 1969 1500 coupé is a reminder of Volkswagen's policy that, 'if it works, don't fix it'. Externally, it is little different from the cars that preceded it, but beneath the engine lid sits one of Volkswagen's finest ever power units.

above the engine in Beetle fashion, rather than on the nose of the crankshaft. Top speed was increased to about 82mph, but this was partly due to the final drive ratio being raised from 4.375:1 to 4.125:1, to allow more relaxed cruising.

Overall, the 1500 Karmann-Ghia was radically different from the preceding models. Besides its improved performance, there were important detail changes to the chassis. Powerful disc brakes were introduced on the front, the rear track was increased, and the rear suspension was modified to include an equaliser spring designed to minimise the car's tendency to oversteer. The spring, which provides assistance to the torsion bars under load, runs transversely under the rear luggage bay, is connected to both axle tubes by rods and levers, and is secured to

the inner wing panels by rubber-bushed brackets.

Other modifications included a change from single-circuit to dual-circuit brakes, four-stud rather than five-stud road wheels, a new 'safety' interior mirror designed to detach itself automatically in the event of a collision, soft plastic switchgear in black to prevent reflections in the windscreen, and a wood-grain finish for the dashboard.

The three-speed semi-automatic gearbox introduced as an option for 1968 was similar in principle to the system used on the Sportomatic version of the Porsche 911 and, of course, on the Beetle. There was no clutch pedal but you still had to move the gear lever to change gear, the clutch being operated pneumatically. A vacuum control valve on the left-hand side of the engine bay was operated in turn by a solenoid which engaged a switch at the base of the gear lever, allowing the driver to change gear without a clutch pedal.

Although the semi-automatic system was reliable, engine performance and fuel consumption suffered, so this version was unpopular. The real advantage of the semi-automatic cars was their double-jointed

Massive wrap-round reflectors are typical of how safety-conscious motor manufacturers had become by the late 1960s and early 1970s. This style of tail lighting arrived for 1971.

driveshafts (*à la* Porsche), and an additional semi-trailing arm which improved the handling by minimising still further the possibility of wheel 'tuck-in' during hard cornering.

In the same year, 12-volt electrics replaced the old six-volt system, and hazard warning lights were standard. There was a larger exterior mirror and 'safety' door handles with trigger releases on the inside. The fuel filler moved from under the bonnet to behind a flap on the right-hand front wing, the combined ignition/starter switch was integrated into the right-hand side of the steering column, and the bonnet release knob was moved to a new position within the glovebox.

After all these changes the 1969 model year was something of a disappointment. A plastic pull-ring for operating the fuel filler flap was fitted below the dashboard on the right-hand side, and radial-ply tyres were standard – but otherwise the car remained essentially unaltered.

For 1970 again there were no major changes because the Karmann-Ghia had by now become relatively sophisticated and worldwide sales continued at a healthy pace. The car handled exceptionally well, but where performance and fuel economy were concerned the Karmann was rapidly losing ground to

the competition, despite the recent introduction of the more powerful 1500 engine.

More power came in the shape of the 50bhp 1600 engine for the 1971 model year. The air-cooled flat-four was 'bored out' to 1584cc, and it had a stronger crankcase and a more efficient aluminium oil cooler – but the most effective modification was to the cylinder heads. Instead of the traditional and restrictive single-port layout, the heads were modified to a twin-port configuration which allowed the engine to 'breathe' more easily and rev more freely. Top speed rose to around 83mph, but despite this welcome gain the new engine was still understressed by the standards of the

When the fuel filler was moved from its traditional position under the bonnet to the right-hand front wing for the 1968 model year, Karmann applied typical attention to detail by fitting a plastic flap to prevent fuel being splashed on the paintwork.

day. The MG Midget, for example, produced 65bhp from just 1275cc and the Alpine-Renault 1600S developed 138bhp from just 1565cc, so Karmann-Ghia owners were still not in a position to outgun the 'opposition' in the performance stakes.

Other modifications for this year included wrap-round, angular front indicators, larger tail lights (they were nearly 10in tall) that incorporated reversing lights, improved door sealing rubbers, and hair-cord carpets to replace rubber mats in the front footwells. A VW 1600 badge was also applied to the engine lid.

As production was to end in 1974 to make way for the Scirocco, the 1972 model year was the last in which any significant modifications were made. There was a new matt black dashboard incorporating larger instruments, a 'safety' four-spoke steering wheel with a large, flat, central horn pad (designed to decrease the likelihood of serious chest injuries in the event of an accident) and improved seats. In addition, the rear light clusters were enlarged yet again (they were now 14in tall), there were larger, stronger 'Europa' bumpers with optional overriders, and the rear wings were slightly modified in shape. A nickel-plated silencer became standard for 1973.

From its debut in 1955 to its demise in 1974, the coupé was modified in thousands of ways, but many of the changes were minute. The car's specification also differed considerably from one market to another.

Although major changes were announced in August at the beginning of each new model year, anomalies were always bound to occur, and sometimes a car with a genuine factory specification may appear to be 'wrong' for the model year in which it was made. There are many reasons for this, but usually it occurred when components from one model year were carried through to the next simply to use up 'old' stocks. Then there were Volkswagen's more conservative customers who disliked certain modifications and had their new cars changed by the dealers to the previous year's specification. And there are the inevitable 'rogue' cars whose specification almost defies explanation. It was sometimes the case that a car destined to be shipped to one market found its way to another, and therefore appears to have the 'wrong' specification.

Driving impressions

In one way, the Karmann coupé flatters to deceive. It was one of the most advanced styling exercises of its day, yet beneath its curvaceous, feminine lines lay the engine and running gear of an underpowered saloon car. However, it is important to put the car into context. During the first decade of the coupé's production, there was no shortage of choice in the medium-sized sports car market, and Karmann decided not to enter it.

Britain offered the Austin-Healey 100, Morgan, MG TF (or MGA from 1955), Triumph TR and, from 1958, Lotus Elite. In Italy, Fiat produced its 1500S and 1600S models with disc brakes (from 1961) and 120mph top speed potential. And in Germany, Porsche had the sports 1500/1600 class pretty well wrapped up with the 356.

Derek Frow's beautifully original 1972 coupé basks in spring sunshine. Two years after this delectable car was built, the Karmann-Ghia would be no more. By the early 1970s, safety played a large part in car design, which is why Karmann fitted larger tail lights and stronger bumpers. This was also an era in which Volkswagen started searching frantically for a successor to the Beetle and the Karmann-Ghia. The writing was on the wall for both.

Incorporating built-in reversing lights and reflectors, the late tail light clusters are almost 14in tall. Although larger 'Europa' bumpers were fitted to late models, at least the Karmann was spared the ignominy of having rubber 'cow-catchers' *à la* MGB and Midget.

From Karmann's, and indeed Volkswagen's, point of view there was little to be gained in trying to compete. Porsche had developed the Beetle engine for better performance and eventually progressed from pushrod engines into sophisticated four-cam units. For Karmann to have been taken seriously as a manufacturer of fast sports cars, it would have had to have taken the same route, or go to the prohibitive expense of developing a brand new power unit.

Instead, the Karmann-Ghia was marketed as an alternative to the humble Beetle saloon, and for good reason: it also drove like one. Naturally, there were differences between the two cars, but the one most noted by journalists was that the Karmann felt like a sports car even if it did not go like one. The fact that a standard 30bhp Beetle saloon was quicker than an MG TC escaped their attention, but that's another story.

Like the Beetle, one of the most attractive features of the coupé was its exceptional build quality. Even after perhaps 100,000 miles of hard driving, it is quite remarkable that so many could remain in such good condition, mechanically and cosmetically. Everything about the car was impeccably, but simply, finished. And true to Volkswagen form, its concept remained the same to the end.

Karmann owners soon got used to the idea of their steeds starting first time, every time, despite the infamous six-volt electrical system. Unlike many high-performance cars of the period, the sparking plugs never oiled up, the clutch was light and silky, and pulling away from rest was not the fraught affair that so many had experienced with thoroughbreds.

Typically firm, the broad and reasonably contoured seats were comfortable, particularly on long journeys. They could be adjusted by up to 4in fore and aft, but they were low-slung, and many shorter drivers experienced difficulty in seeing clearly over the top of the steering wheel. With slim roof pillars, a curved panoramic windscreen (the Beetle's was flat until 1964) and large glass area, all-round visibility was exceptionally good.

For a two-seater, luggage space was more than adequate, but no-one could pretend that the car was ever in the Grand Touring class. It was most certainly a touring car, but never grand. One recurring criticism of the cabin was the inadequate ventilation system, which, without quarterlights in the door windows, was wholly reliant upon two controls under the dashboard feeding air to the windscreen and to the rear window. There was no ventilation at foot or knee level. Cool, fresh air was provided only by opening the door windows.

Massive wrap-round indicators did little, if anything, to improve the car's appearance for the 1971 model year.

The uniquely curvaceous nose is one of the car's most endearing features. From 1959, the intake grille had three horizontal slats instead of two.

Throughout the production life of the Karmann, no-one had heard of the word 'ergonomics', but the coupé was at least competent. The layout of the controls was simple and there were few of them, but drivers brought up on conventional cars found the bottom-hinged pedals awkward. Seasoned Volkswagen customers did not. Indeed, if there was any criticism of the pedals, it was that they were slightly offset to the left on right-hand drive versions. But the main drawback to this was that, after many years, the driver's seat had a tendency to sag on the right-hand side as a result of the uneven distribution of the driver's weight.

When the engine was fired up from cold, noise levels inside the cabin were relatively high, but they decreased as the flat-four warmed up. Any air-cooled engine tends to be louder than a water-cooled one, but Volkswagen went a long way to reduce noise levels by introducing better soundproofing materials, and by reducing the speed of the cooling fan (by using a larger dynamo pulley and a smaller crankshaft pulley) on the 34bhp 1200 engine in 1960.

Driving a Karmann always was, and remains, a most rewarding experience – despite a weight increase over the Beetle of around 180lb. Comparing the two cars in 1961, *The Autocar* commented: 'It was at medium to high road speeds that the increased performance was most evident. For example, 40-60mph in top gear required 19.5sec, whereas the time for the saloon was 25.2sec. Similarly, when accelerating from rest to 60mph, the corresponding figures were 26.5sec and 32.1sec, and the mean maximum speed of a Karmann-Ghia was 77mph – an increase of 5mph over that of the saloon.'

The coupé's higher performance was entirely due to its superior wind-cheating shape. Although no figures are officially available, the drag co-efficient is thought to be in the region of 0.44-0.45, compared

Well-contoured and deeply padded, the bucket seats offered excellent lateral support and, being typically firm, were most comfortable over long distances.

For 1972, the dashboard received a matt black finish and for safety reasons the padded four-spoke steering wheel had a much larger centre section, alterations which the Karmann-Ghia shared with the Beetle.

with the Beetle's 0.49. *The Autocar*'s fuel consumption over 1132 miles was 31.2mpg, which is more or less what a Beetle owner could expect in the early 1960s.

Much has been said over the years about the roadholding and handling of rear-engined Volkswagens, and most of the criticism is complete drivel. With 59 per cent of the car's weight concentrated at the rear, there is certainly a natural tendency to oversteer, but those who learned to enjoy the delights of 'opposite-lock' motoring soon discovered that Karmanns and Beetles were both safer and faster through corners than contemporary understeering, nose-heavy, front-engined cars.

Rear wheel 'tuck-in' could be a problem because of the action of the swing axles, but this only ever

occurred at extreme speeds. The driving method required is best summed up by Denis Jenkinson in his book *Porsche Past & Present* (Gentry Books, 1983), in which he describes Richard von Frankenburg's technique for conducting a Porsche 356 around corners: 'Frankenburg's method of control was to provoke a tail slide sooner than the car wanted to do it naturally, and then neutralise it instantly by correcting the steering: before the car could react to this steering input, he would provoke it again into oversteer.'

Those who failed to learn this technique branded the car's handling as unsatisfactory, and their negative chimes have been repeated in parrot-fashion ever since. To be fair to *Autocar*, that magazine's road testers, writing in 1965, said: 'Oversteer is only noticed in really hard cornering, and is easily controlled.' But journalists were still apt to write of oversteer as being something that was undesirable, although Volkswagen enthusiasts never discovered quite why.

The tendency to oversteer had more to do with

Because of changes to the air cleaner in 1966, the battery was moved from the right-hand side to the left. Twin-port heads were introduced on the 1600 for 1971 and helped the flat-four engine to breathe more freely.

the standard, skinny, crossply tyres than with the design of the independent rear suspension or engine position, and anyone running a Karmann-Ghia today would do well to fit radials. However, Volkswagen had no option but to take notice of the criticism: after it fitted an equaliser spring to the rear suspension and widened the track upon the introduction of the 1500 model, the Karmann-Ghia and the Beetle turned into neutral handlers. When double-jointed driveshafts and semi-trailing arms arrived on the semi-automatic models, the cars even understeered, which to a large extent took the fun out of driving them.

One great advantage of rear weight bias, incidentally, was that traction on slippery surfaces was of the highest order, and has not been surpassed by a

37

By 1972, the last year in which significant modifications were made to the coupé, it was a well-mannered, civilised and even sophisticated car, but **there was no disguising its pedestrian performance. Even with progressive power increases, the air-cooled flat-four was no match for the competition.**

two-wheel drive vehicle to this day, except perhaps by the current breed of rear-engined Porsches.

Handling aside, the steering became legendary for its lightness and precision. The gearbox was completely vice-free, especially after synchromesh was introduced on first gear in 1960. Bryan Hanrahan, writing in *Modern Motor* in 1967, reckoned that it was 'one of the slickest pieces of machinery of its kind yet devised', and the gearbox came in for similar praise from every journalist. Braking was always fade-free even before front discs were fitted for 1967 but, like the Beetle, the Karmann-Ghia had a tendency to lock its front wheels under heavy braking on wet surfaces, a trait of all rear-engined cars before anti-lock braking was conceived.

The real Achilles' heel of the Karmann-Ghia was its astonishingly awful six-volt lighting system. Driving at night in the late 1950s and early 1960s was only possible at high speeds at all because the roads were relatively free of traffic, but no-one in his right mind would rely on the headlamps to light the way ahead safely at anything above 45mph. Today, halogen bulbs are readily available and dramatically improve matters, but in recent times many Karmann-Ghia owners have understandably converted their cars to the later 12-volt specification.

For all its faults, the Karmann-Ghia coupé was desirable because it was so different from everything else. Its styling, reliability and durability were strong selling points. It was easy to drive and gave good fuel economy, and owners ran their cars secure in the knowledge that Volkswagen's international servicing and spare parts service was second to none. There was no radiator to boil over or run dry, no water hoses to split open, and it would always start regardless of weather conditions. Quite simply, there was nothing else like the Karmann-Ghia.

THE CONVERTIBLE

The most sought after Karmann–Ghia and the least affordable of the entire air-cooled Volkswagen range, the upmarket convertible version was produced in low numbers from the beginning of August 1957 (from chassis number 1 600 440) and the majority were exported to North America. First exhibited to the public at the Frankfurt Motor Show and based, like the coupé, on the modified Beetle 1200 chassis and standard running gear, the convertible represented a combination of Italian chic and German build quality.

Karmann was used to coping with the problems of soft-top construction and took considerable steps to strengthen the body against the loss of torsional stiffness caused by removing the roof. There were exceptionally strong panel sections incorporated into the sills and drilled to reduce weight, strengthening

Launched for the 1958 model year, the convertible was heavier, costlier and slightly slower than its 'tin-top' sister, but captured the imagination of those who longed for a two-seater alternative to the Beetle cabriolet.

panels around the rear bulkhead, and further reinforcing panels either side of the back seat around the area where the hood folds away.

The hood was designed to be simple in operation so that one person could easily open or close it. By turning a handle above the rear view mirror, two retaining claws were released from the top of the steel windscreen frame and the hood could then be pushed backwards and folded neatly into place. To prevent it from flapping about in the wind, a hood bag was provided, and secured with press studs.

A symbol of the carefree sixties, the convertible offered wind-in-the-hair motoring Volkswagen style for those who could afford the high price and did not mind modest performance.

The hood, which took two of Karmann's craftsmen four hours to make, folds away neatly in the rear luggage compartment. The leatherette seats were piped with vinyl on early cars.

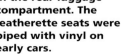

Raising the hood merely involved turning the handle to lock the catches into place, and in typical Karmann fashion it fitted perfectly. So beautifully made that it took two experienced craftsmen four hours to make, the Karmann's hood was in stark contrast to those fitted to the majority of cheap British sports cars of the period. The latter were almost always made of a single layer of canvas (with or without a headlining) stretched over a crude and ill-fitting metal framework, whereas the Karmann's hood was a bespoke work of art which only rarely leaked and was always draught-free. The typically detailed Volkswagen handbook included no fewer than seven different instructions for opening the hood and five for closing it.

The hood consisted of a mohair outer skin, a woolcloth headlining and a horsehair filling between the two. The collapsible metal framework was held together with screws and there were sturdy wooden bows at the front and back. Unlike the Beetle

After August 1959, right-hand drive versions of the convertible and coupé became available, mainly for the British and Swedish markets.

Perfectly poised for continental touring, Derek Frow's Ferrite Brown convertible is now in concours condition after a seven-year restoration.

cabriolet, the Karmann-Ghia convertible's rear window was plastic rather than glass, and the fact that it was a little smaller than the coupé's made rearward vision less satisfactory. The plastic window could also become scratched and difficult to see through, but in that respect it was no different from most convertibles.

Volkswagen's original sales literature for the convertible pointed out that the seat covers and interior panels were made in a 'non-fading' material, but the passage of nearly 40 years shows that even the normally restrained marketing people in Wolfsburg could occasionally be economical with the truth. 'It is

Because the rear window was originally made of plastic, it tends to become scratched and difficult to see through.

In one sense, it is a pity that the hood was made so well because driving a convertible in poor weather feels little different from a coupé.

For security reasons, the vulnerable convertible differs from the coupé in having a lockable bonnet release.

the lively, elegant car that one always dreamed of,' says the sales brochure, '…modest price, high performance and of the best breeding.' Few would dispute the latter claim, but 'modest price' and 'high performance' are most definitely open to question. When the convertible first came to Britain in 1958, its hefty £1395 price put it on a par with cars like the MGA Twin-Cam, Austin-Healey 3000 and Daimler SP250, all of which had far superior performance – even if their build quality was poorer.

By the mid-1960s, extravagant claims had been dropped in favour of the legendary self-deprecating advertising campaigns that provide so much amusement today. One American advertisement

In stark contrast to the crude hoods fitted to the majority of inexpensive British sporting cars, the convertible's hood was made from an outer skin of mohair, a cloth headlining and a horsehair filling. The Karmann's handbook gives no fewer than 12 instructions for opening and closing it.

The vinyl seats in this 1959 convertible are typical of the period. Although hard-wearing, easy to clean and firm, the lack of lateral support made fast cornering a problem for 'speed merchants'.

Karmann relied heavily on Beetle parts for the interior fittings, but a touch of luxury was provided by the padding over the top of the dashboard.

pointed out that the convertible Karmann-Ghia was not the sports car it looked: 'It is a touring car. It'll do 82mph all day. But don't be misled. It'll also get about 28 miles to a gallon of regular gas. Average 40,000 miles to a set of tyres. The engine is air-cooled, so it can never overheat or freeze. And it won't need tuning between tune-ups.' And the advertisement finally asks: 'Does that sound like a sports car to you?'

Like its tin-top sister, the convertible was something of an enigma because it did not fit into a convenient pigeon hole. It had fine looks, it was exceptionally well screwed together, and it was endowed with good road manners, but performance was lacking and, unlike the majority of sporting cars, it

For approximately every four coupés made there was one convertible, a ratio reflected at club gatherings today.

The semi-circular horn ring on the steering wheel was dropped in 1964, the horn being operated by elongated thumb buttons built into the spokes. Curiously, the ring reappeared in 1966.

was reliable and cheap to run. But for once, Volkswagen enthusiasts were not alone in understanding where the car's appeal lay. As one American advertisement put it: 'A Volkswagen Karmann-Ghia does not have a lot of chrome or senseless decorations. It doesn't need them. The secret of its elegance is in its simple lines, its lively form.'

The car looked pretty whether the top was up or down and its styling is far from dated today. It is difficult to imagine why the Mk1 Golf Cabriolet which eventually replaced the Karmann convertible should be thought of as an improvement but, in all probability, enthusiasts in the future will look upon it with the same degree of affection.

Production modifications......................

As the convertible was so similar to the coupé, it was treated to the same year-on-year design changes described in the previous chapter (starting on page 25). However, the hood on the convertible was changed

during the 1969 model year to include a rear window made of glass rather than plastic, and the front hood catches were made smaller and controlled by levers on each side of the windscreen frame.

Driving impressions...........................

It goes without saying that driving the convertible Type 1 is virtually the same as driving the hard-top coupé, but because the convertible is a little heavier (thanks to its additional body strengthening panels) it is also slightly slower – around 2mph on top speed and 1sec or so in 0-60mph acceleration. But the differences in performance are almost imperceptible, even to seasoned 'boy racers'.

The point of the convertible was to offer fresh air fans a two-seater alternative to the four-seater Beetle cabriolet, and this concept worked very well. With the hood raised, the lines of the car remained virtually the same as those of the coupé – from a distance it is actually difficult to tell one from another. But with the

These comfortable seats are similar to those fitted to the Volkswagen Type 4 saloon launched in 1968, while American-specification cars also had head restraints.

From mid-1969, the rear window was made of glass rather than plastic.

The large wrap-round front indicators somehow detracted from the convertible's elegant styling to a greater extent than on the coupé.

A 'wood-grain' dashboard was introduced on the 1500 for 1967. Considering that Karmann was a bespoke coachbuilder, it is surprising that it did not come sooner.

45

The last right-hand drive convertible (chassis number 144 2668 285) was manufactured in February 1974 and came to Britain the following year. Restored in 1989 by Luke Theochari, it is fitted with non-original 'Marathon' Beetle road wheels.

Radial tyres may not impress concours judges, but at least they enable the owner of this 1966 convertible to drive more safely to and from such events.

hood folded down, the convertible looks even better. There are no awkward corners and even the top of the windscreen frame is neatly finished, unlike that of the 1303 Beetle cabriolet which dominates the whole of the car's frontal appearance because of the large size of the panoramic windscreen.

In one sense, it is a pity that the hood was so well made because driving a convertible with it raised is little different from driving a coupé. The wet climate

helped to keep sales low in Britain, but those who were brave enough to buy the rag-top were always grateful that the hood fitted so well and was so weatherproof that it rarely gave cause for concern, even in a blizzard. Hoods have also stood the test of time exceptionally well, except where they have been attacked by mindless vandals.

One of the classic problems usually associated with convertibles is the body flexing and scuttle shake

To some, the 'Europa' bumpers, large overriders and tall tail lights of 1972 cars did even less for the convertible's styling than they did for the coupé's.

Convertibles continued to be popular in sun-soaked California throughout the last year of production, but by the end of 1974 the Osnabrück assembly lines had been turned over to Scirocco production for Volkswagen.

caused by the loss of torsional rigidity inherent in removing the roof, but the Karmann-Ghia's steel body is so rigid that these problems arise only in exceptional circumstances.

Writing in the British specialist Volkswagen magazine, *Safer Motoring* (now *VW Motoring*), Peter Noad commented in his road test of a secondhand convertible: 'No draughts or excessive noise intruded, and the only indication when driving of the existence of a soft-top was a trace of shake on very bumpy roads. All cars rely on the roof to add rigidity to the body structure, and it is to be expected that convertibles will exhibit some vibration or scuttle shake. In the case of the VW this was only noticeable

on particularly rough-surfaced minor roads.'

However, the car's ability to remain vibration-free has as much to do with the strength of the Volkswagen chassis as it has with the reinforced bodyshell. Almost unbreakable, the firm all-independent torsion bar suspension allows the Karmann-Ghia to be driven nearly as quickly over a rough field as on a smooth motorway, and it retains its feeling of tautness after many thousands of miles.

During the 1960s, when the convertible was at the height of its popularity, there was no shortage of choice in the sports car market. To some, it is surprising that the car survived such a long production run of 17 years. By contrast, the two-seater MGB

47

In contrast to the bulbous 1303 Beetle cabriolet, it is particularly apparent on this 1970 car how the windscreen frame was skilfully integrated into the overall styling of the Karmann-Ghia.

By 1970, when Darin Frow's car was made, the convertible had acquired 12-volt electrics, a little more weight and a 50bhp 1600 engine, but in essence it remained the same as ever.

roadster – launched in 1962 and produced for 18 years – was a better buy, on paper at least. Right from the start, the British car had front disc brakes (which the Karmann did not receive until four years later), a 1798cc engine developing 95bhp and an overdrive top gear as an option. As early as 1962, the MG was good for over 100mph whereas the Karmann-Ghia, which at that time had the 1192cc engine developing just 34bhp, struggled to reach 80mph.

The roadholding capabilities of both cars were considered by many to be roughly equal and average fuel consumption figures were similar. The British car enjoyed some success in motor sport and continues on its winning way in European historic rallies today, but the Karmann convertible was only rarely seen in minor sporting events despite the potential for tuning offered by Okrasa and other specialist companies. But both cars had a very healthy following in the American market, where they were bought for different reasons and different purposes.

Today, the MGB and Karmann-Ghia both remain as popular as ever on both sides of the Atlantic, but while the former has been given a new lease of life as the RV8, the Karmann-Ghia convertible has been allowed to grow old gracefully. It does not enjoy a cult following to the same degree as the Beetle, and never will. But for those who are tuned in to wind-in-the-hair motoring Karmann style, nothing else will do.

THE TYPE 3

For a car that remained virtually unchanged throughout its brief production run of just eight years, the Type 3 Karmann-Ghia has been given an extraordinary number of names. In the Volkswagen numbering hierarchy, the basic left-hand drive version was a Type 343 (or 345 if it had a sunroof), or a Type 34 to simplify matters. In Germany it was referred to as the 'Grosse Karmann-Ghia' or large Karmann-Ghia, in Britain it was known as the 'Razor-edge', and in the USA (to which it was never officially exported) it was called the 'European Ghia'. No doubt there were equally bewildering titles given to it in various other countries as well.

Because the original coupé was known as the Type 1 after the saloon on which it was based, I have chosen to call the later car the Type 3 Karmann-Ghia for the simple reason that it was based on Volkswagen's Type 3 saloon/variant.

To a completely new body design, the Type 3

If the Type 1 was feminine and pretty, the Type 3 was elegant and aggressive. This 1964 example is owned by Andy Holmes.

Karmann-Ghia relied on the same formula that had led to the success of the Type 1: Volkswagen mechanicals, Ghia styling and Karmann craftsmanship. Originally, it was intended as the successor to the Type 1 coupé in the same way that the Type 3 saloon was proposed as a successor to the Beetle, but things did not turn out that way. First shown to the public at the Frankfurt Motor Show in September 1961, the Type 3 had radical styling and received a mixed reaction. An elegant convertible version appeared at the same time, but plans to put it into production were shelved because the body lacked sufficient torsional stiffness. Just two prototypes were built and one survives today in the Karmann museum.

Ghia's Sergio Sartorelli had drawn the lines of the

Little changed between the development stage and the production version, the Type 3 was first shown at the Frankfurt Motor Show in September 1961. The foglamps are closer to the headlamps on this early prototype.

new coupé as early as 1958, and those who considered the styling of the new car unacceptable can be grateful that Ghia's other design exercises did not get much beyond drawing board stage. Whereas the Type 1 was curvaceous and easy on the eye, the Type 3 had an aggressive appearance which to many was an acquired taste. If the Type 1 was the Johann Strauss of the Volkswagen world, the Type 3 was the Gustav Mahler. Both had their merits, but the former would always appeal to a much larger audience.

Aesthetically, the body was nicely balanced with a long nose and rear end, and the roof, with its slim pillars and large glass area, gave an overall appearance of lithe elegance. Both the windscreen and rear window were sharply curved and steeply raked, and in that respect were well in advance of their British and European contemporaries. From a three-quarter rear view there was a look of the Chevrolet Corvair, but the sharp swage line running almost unbroken from front to rear – a bone of contention for critics – 'squared-up' the body in an era when rounded curves were more in vogue.

The most damning criticism of the styling was reserved for the quad-headlight layout and the swage line at the top of the front panel. Apart from the headlights, the latter made the front of the car look

almost indistinguishable from its rear. Clearly, the designers were pandering to American taste, but it was perhaps not generally realised at the time that Americans buy European cars for their distinctive European styling and not for their pseudo-American looks, which is why the Type 1 continued to sell long after the demise of the Type 3.

Naturally, the concept of the Type 3 was similar to that of the Type 1, although it was an altogether bigger car: wider, longer and higher than the Type 1, and at 2006lb (dry weight), 264lb heavier. There were two seats with an occasional rear seat, the engine was placed in the tail, and torsion bar suspension was used front and rear. The dashboard was slightly different from the Type 1's and followed the Type 3 saloon in having large gauges for fuel (left), speedometer (centre) and clock (right).

The front suspension was slightly different from the conventional arrangement on the Beetle and Type 1 coupé. From the beginning, the Type 3 was fitted with ball joints rather than king and link pins, and the torsion bars, which run across the full width of the front 'axle', crossed over in the middle. The lower of the two cylindrical axle tubes contained the anti-roll bar, rather than having a separate bar outside the tube in Type 1 fashion.

The Type 3 was propelled by a brand new 1493cc engine with a bore and stroke of 83mm × 69mm and developing a maximum 45bhp at 3800rpm. The basic

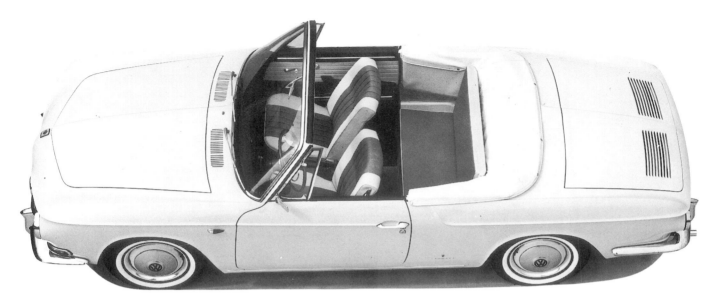

A lack of torsional stiffness in the bodyshell ensured that production of a convertible version of the Type 3 was shelved. This is one of just two prototypes built by Karmann in 1961.

The Type 3 Karmann-Ghia was based on the 1500 Type 3 saloon/variant range launched in 1961. The prototype convertible version of the four-seater saloon did not go into production.

layout of this unit was, of course, the same as ever. The overhead valves were still opened by pushrods driven by a single camshaft placed below the crankshaft at a time when many of the world's manufacturers of sporting cars were turning to more efficient overhead camshafts. Volkswagen also persisted with single-port cylinder heads on the Type 3 until the 1968 model year.

This conservatism was perfectly understandable if the object was to maintain the Beetle's reputation for reliability and longevity, but it has been a constant source of wonder to Volkswagen enthusiasts that the

company did not fit twin-port cylinder heads sooner, at least to the more sporting cars in its range. After all, the specialist German tuning company, Okrasa, had been offering this performance conversion from the mid-1950s, with no detriment to reliability. However, Volkswagen was slow to change, and by the time it caught on to the idea it was getting just a little late.

The crankcase was from the stronger 1200 Beetle engine introduced in 1960, and there was a brand new crankshaft, but the biggest break from tradition was in the position of the cooling fan on the nose of the crankshaft instead of above the crankcase. Although it

By the late 1950s and early 1960s, Karmann had abandoned water colour illustrations in its sales literature in favour of more conventional photographs. The company was so confident of producing a convertible that it was included in the original brochures.

was smaller in diameter than the Beetle item, it increased the airflow to the engine thanks to its superior shape, but the main advantage was that it reduced the engine's overall height to just 16in.

This allowed the Type 3 to have a second 'boot' for luggage. It is true that the rear luggage bay could take little more than a medium-sized suitcase, but it was still an ingenious piece of design which no other manufacturer could boast. Access to the engine was through a lift-up panel in the floor of the boot, a feature shared by the Type 3 saloon, the Type 4 (launched in 1968) and the third-generation Transporter (from 1979).

The 1500 engine was initially fitted with a single Solex 32 PHIN horizontal (or sidedraught) carburettor. Despite the weight of the car, this was good enough to take the Type 3 above 80mph and to cover 0-60mph in around 18sec. This was an improvement over the Type 1, but it still was not in the sports car class.

To be fair, the Type 3 was not intended to be a sports car, for here was another unique Volkswagen hybrid that just did not fit into an accepted pigeon hole. At first, British customers were not impressed either with the price (the hefty £1281 was double the

cost of a 1200 Beetle) or the fact that right-hand drive versions were unavailable until the 1964 model year.

At the time of the car's launch, there was no shortage of choice for anyone in the market for a two-seater tourer in the Karmann-Ghia mould. The pretty Alfa Romeo Giulietta Sprint was similar in concept and developed an impressive 80bhp from just 1290cc, good enough for a genuine 100mph. Lancia in 1962 launched the Flavia Coupé, a full four-seater which shared a quad-headlight layout with the Karmann-Ghia, but Pininfarina had made a rather less revolutionary stab than Ghia at integrating them into the overall styling. In Britain the new Lotus Elan, unveiled in 1962, shared some distant similarity with the Volkswagen in having a backbone chassis and all-independent suspension, but the Lotus had a free-revving 1558cc twin overhead camshaft engine that was capable of propelling it beyond 105mph, and there was no way Volkswagen could compete with that kind of performance.

Compared with these sports cars, the Karmann-Ghia merely created an illusion of power and appealed to an 'understanding' and specialist audience. For Volkswagen, the company reached a turning point with the launch of the Type 3 saloon and Karmann-

Ghia, intended respectively as successors to the Beetle and the Type 1 coupé. Sales of the Type 3 – 42,498 were built between March 1962 and July 1969 – were nowhere near as low as some commentators like to believe, but were poor in comparison with what Volkswagen had expected and, indeed, with what it was used to.

Throughout the early 1960s, Ghia continued to submit designs for alternative bodies on the Type 3 platform chassis, but all were turned down. In 1963 a Swiss engineer, Hermann Klaue, proposed a Beetle successor with a water-cooled 1.5-litre engine and front-wheel drive, and had the project found favour the Volkswagen Scirocco may well have replaced the Type 1 Karmann-Ghia a great deal sooner than 1974.

Instead, Volkswagen turned towards Porsche for help in designing a new car, and between them they came up with the Volkswagen Type 4. It was Volkswagen's first proper unitary construction saloon car, utilising MacPherson strut and coil spring suspension rather than torsion bars and, with a new 1700cc engine, giving sufficient performance to put it on an equal footing with its competitors. In both saloon and variant forms the Type 4 had masses of luggage space because, like the Type 3, it had its cooling fan mounted at the rear of the engine. In theory it had all the credentials to become a successful family saloon.

Highly unconventional styling ensured that the Type 4 was not a success, but Volkswagen chief Heinz Nordhoff died on 12 April 1968 and never saw the car make its public debut. In his absence, the Type 3 Karmann-Ghia continued in production, but for less than a further 18 months. It was replaced by the VW-Porsche 914, another two-seater sporting car, but one based on the Type 4 saloon. Torsion bar suspension was, at last, on the way out. Post-Nordhoff, the writing was clearly on the wall for the cars of 'his' era.

53

The frontal aspect, particularly the quad-headlamp layout and sharp 'eyebrow' swage line above, made sure that the styling was always a talking point.

A series of horizontal louvres in the engine lid ensured that the engine's cooling fan was fed with enough air.

Round rear lights contrasted with the banana-shaped items fitted to the Type 1. The 1500S badge indicates that this is a twin-carburettor model, introduced for the 1964 model year.

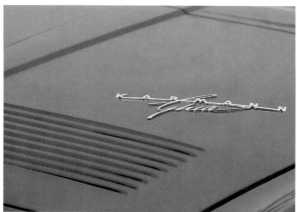

From the beginning of production, the Type 3 was fitted with flat hub caps rather than the domed variety which saw service on the Type 1 coupé, Beetle and Transporter.

The Type 3 Karmann-Ghia should have been more successful. Its credentials were impeccable, and in many respects it was Volkswagen's best product of the 1960s, but like so many cars that would take its place over the next 20 years it fell between the devil and the deep blue sea.

The styling certainly played a part in the Type 3's downfall but the historically important relationship between Volkswagen and Porsche almost certainly had a more significant role. Potential customers of both companies were confronted with a difficult choice in the showroom. The Type 3 was an expensive Volkswagen, and a little more money could buy a Porsche 356, with better performance and a more prestigious badge – so Volkswagen lost out.

The same marketing problem arose with the VW-Porsche 914 and 916. A 'proper' Porsche, the 911, cost very little more to buy and no-one able to afford a 911 would settle for anything less, especially if it wore a Volkswagen badge. The 914 was an

Front luggage space is more generous than in the Type 1 coupé.

An alloy 'birth certificate' giving information about the car's weights sits on the inside of the right-hand inner wing close to the fuel filler neck.

exceptionally good car, but it was the 'wrong' side of the Volkswagen to be a Porsche. In more recent times, both the Audi-built Porsche 924 and Volkswagen Corrado have fallen victim to the same overlap between the products of Stuttgart and Wolfsburg.

A Volkswagen is a People's car. Most of the people could not afford a Type 3, but those who could found it a magnificent and graceful carriage built to exacting standards by people who cared about 'old world' craftsmanship. Those who drove Type 3 Karmann-Ghias understood all that, but unfortunately there were not enough of them.

Production modifications......................

As with the Beetle and the Type 1 coupé, major changes to the Type 3 were announced each year at the beginning of August. Mechanically, it adopted all the modifications made to the Type 3 saloon, but there were comparatively few by Beetle standards.

A right-hand drive version became available for the British market for the 1964 model year, when the 1500 engine was fitted with twin Solex 32 PDSIT-2 and -3 carburettors – and known as the 1500S engine. The compression ratio was raised from 7.8:1 to 8.5:1 and consequently power was boosted to 54bhp at 4200rpm. This was arguably the very best air-cooled power unit ever produced by Volkswagen and it is a

great pity that it was never installed in the Beetle.

The same year the rotary knob on the backbone tunnel for operating the heating system was replaced by two pull-up handles, the semi-circular horn ring was dropped and replaced by two elongated thumb buttons embedded in the steering wheel spokes, and the cloth interior panels were replaced by washable plastic items. The original steel road wheels, which had narrow slots between the hubs and the rims, were replaced by 'solid' wheels without slots (the optional aluminium alloy wheel trims still came with slots) and the square VW badge on the nose was replaced with the more familiar round item.

For the 1965 model year, the semi-circular horn ring was reintroduced on the steering wheel, the horn itself was mounted externally beneath the bumper and there were two-speed windscreen wipers to replace the former simple rheostat control. With six-volt

Built in an era when curves were in vogue, the clean cut 'Razor-edge', as the Type 3 is known in Britain, looks happiest from the rear.

The oil dipstick is conveniently positioned near the rear panel.

electrics, the speed at which the wipers moved, on either speed setting, was very much dependent upon the condition of the battery. In practice it was difficult to tell the setting from looking at the wipers.

The following year, the 1493cc engine was enlarged to 1584cc, the stroke remaining at 69mm but the cylinder bore increasing from 83mm to 85.5mm. Unfortunately, though, this engine was no more powerful than the 1500 it replaced, because the compression ratio was reduced to 7.7:1 to allow for the use of poor quality fuels in some markets. Maximum power remained unchanged at 54bhp, but with the 1600 it was developed at 4000rpm rather than 4200rpm.

In addition, the 1966 model saw the introduction of disc brakes at the front, ventilated four-stud road wheels with optional alloy trims (which were vented to match the wheels), and improvements to the interior. Reshaped door armrests, a vanity mirror on the underside of the passenger's sun visor, and tough hair-cord carpet (in place of rubber mats) in the front footwells were further improvements.

Along with the Type 1 coupé, the Type 3 was fitted with 12-volt electrics for the 1967 model year, a move that gave a boost to the much criticised headlamps, not to mention the car's ability to start on cold mornings.

A safety interior mirror, designed to detach itself

Since the cooling fan was mounted on the nose of the crankshaft, the engine was a mere 16in in height, allowing for an additional luggage space in the rear above the engine.

automatically in the event of an accident, was fitted as standard equipment, but a heated rear window became an attractive optional extra. To improve safety further, the single-circuit braking was replaced by a dual circuit system.

Inside the car, cable locks were integrated into the front seat backrests and operated by plastic handles built into the sides of the backrests near the top. The advantage of this modification was simply to allow the backrests to be tilted forward, without having to bend

A more sporting dashboard for the Type 3 has a clock and fuel gauge flanking the central speedometer. The strange 'dial' to the left of the radio is the radio speaker. The pedals are offset to the left on right-hand drive cars.

A combination of Volkswagen austerity and Porsche-type luxury, the Type 3's interior is comfortable and spacious.

No-one had heard of 'ergonomics' in the mid-1960s, but the gear lever, heater controls and handbrake lever were all well-placed.

down to release the levers at the base of the seats. In addition, the seats were modified to give better lateral support, the handbrake was made shorter, and the gear lever was repositioned and given a narrower 'gate'. The door locking mechanism was modified: instead of pushing a handle on the interior door panel forwards and backwards, a slim knob was built in to the top of each window sill.

A totally incongruous wood-effect dashboard was also added to the list of standard items introduced for 1967. As bespoke coachbuilders, it is surprising that Karmann did not use wood or wood-effect a lot earlier, but many are glad that they did not.

By 1968, the motoring world had become very different from when the Type 3 was introduced, and safety had become a strong issue on both sides of the Atlantic. To that end, the Type 3 was fitted with a collapsible steering column, the rear view mirror was enlarged, all the dashboard switches were made of soft plastic, and the horn ring had a matt rather than chromed finish.

More important, the 1600 engine was, at last, fitted with twin-port cylinder heads, which allowed the unit to breathe more efficiently, and Bosch electronic fuel injection was available as an option. Also optional was a fully automatic gearbox and, like the semi-automatic Type 1, the Type 3 had the advantage of double-jointed driveshafts and the additional semi-trailing arm rear suspension.

In 1969, its final year of production, hazard

The rear seat is as cramped as the one in the Type 1, but headroom is much more generous.

An opening rear side window was a necessity with such a large glass area, especially as ventilation was poor.

warning lights were introduced, there were slimmer rear lights and flatter hub caps, and the modified rear suspension introduced on the automatic cars of the previous year became standard on the manual gearbox cars. Production came to a halt in July 1969 to make way for the VW-Porsche 914, a car with equally bizarre styling and a similarly short production life, but one which enjoyed greater sales success because it was officially exported to the US.

Driving impressions.............................

Despite the many design similarities between the Type 1 coupé and the Type 3, the latter always felt like a very different sort of motor car. The Type 1 was neat, agile and to a degree sporting, whereas the Type 3 was a larger and heavier car which demanded a slightly different driving technique. It could certainly be hustled around the corners at high speeds, but felt more sedate, more stable and just a little more grand.

Handsome, but never pretty, the Type 3 had a charm of its own. It was one of those cars that was a pleasure to drive after a hard day's work, possessing the ability to wash away aches and pains in the same way

that a modern Jaguar or Mercedes–Benz might.

In common with all other Volkswagens of the period, build quality was beyond doubt and engineering integrity was of the highest possible standard. Simply opening and closing the boot lids or the doors was a pleasure. They neither 'clanked' nor vibrated if slammed shut, and the cabin was so air tight that a window needed to be opened before the doors would close properly, even on ageing high-mileage examples. This was the kind of quality for which German engineering gained its universal and enduring reputation, and just one reason why air-cooled Volkswagens are so highly regarded in the classic car world today.

With its large glass area, the cabin was light and airy, except on hot days when it was light, airy and stuffy. Ventilation was never one of Volkswagen's stronger points (and is not to this day), but at least the Type 3 had opening quarterlights in the door windows, unlike the Type 1. The cabin was also considerably wider than Volkswagen owners had come to expect. For the driver this meant that there was more room for those occasions, now unfortunately long since gone, when spirited driving required flailing arms, purposeful shoulder movements and a broad grin…

Confronting the driver was a large, dished steering

The layout of the 'suitcase' twin-carburettor 1500 engine, one of Volkswagen's best power units, is refreshingly different from the Type 1 engine.

wheel, and a typically austere metal dashboard, about which the continental correspondent of *Cars Illustrated* wrote: 'Once ensconced in the seats, the driver finds himself facing three round dials. He shouldn't congratulate himself too soon. True, there is a highly accurate and very readable speedometer, and a fuel gauge (in a VW!) but that is about the extent of things. Even if we excuse them for eliminating the water temperature dial on obvious grounds, a little more information beyond the all-or-nothing lights would help. The clock is very pleasant but I'd rather see that space occupied by information I can't get just as easily from my wrist.' In other words, there was still no tachometer – and there never would be because Volkswagen just did not consider one necessary.

Again, there were firm seats in true German fashion, giving excellent thigh and back support and, being fully adjustable, enabling even short drivers to find a satisfactory driving position. But not everyone liked firm Germanic seating. In its road test of the 1600 version in the mid-1960s the Australian magazine, *Wheels*, said, 'The upholstery of washable vinyl is porous and the perforated centre section breathes well for summer heat. But it is completely unyielding and sometimes uncomfortable.'

All-round visibility was first class and, because the car was a good deal squarer in shape than the Type 1,

it was easier to judge where the four corners were when it came to parking. Those who failed to assess this accurately rarely allowed themselves to crunch the bodywork a second time, as the most casual glance at a Karmann body panel price list had a more sobering effect on driving ability than any optician or professional driving instructor could hope for.

Behind the seats was the familiar occasional rear seat which, being practically useless for its apparent purpose, folded down to give additional luggage space. For those who needed it there was yet more luggage space in the front and rear boots. Admittedly, the rear boot was a little shallow, but at least there was one. Lined with carpet, both front and rear boots insulated the cabin reasonably well from excessive engine and road noise. Incidentally, because the lift-up engine lid formed the floor of the rear luggage space, the oil dipstick was lengthened and protruded up through the most rearward panel – a practical arrangement which solved the potential problem of checking the oil when the boot was loaded.

By comparison with the 34bhp 1200 Type 1 coupé, the Type 3's 45bhp felt most satisfying. Although the original single-carb engine took around 20sec to reach 60mph from rest, once it was coaxed up to high speed it would stay there all day. Not too much attention should be paid to the claimed top

Like a number of Ghia's design studies in the early 1960s, the attractive 'fastback' version of the Type 3 got no further than the prototype stage.

The fastback's twin headlamps were positioned closely together, a questionable improvement upon the production layout.

speeds of these cars because the majority of road tests carried out by magazines were performed without a fifth wheel, but for the record *Cars Illustrated* recorded 78.9mph for the single carburettor 1500, *Road & Track* came up with a best of 87mph for the twin-carburettor version, and *Modern Motor* managed 94mph from the 1600 model.

In keeping with the rest of the Volkswagen range, one of the most endearing features of the Type 3 was its unusually high top gear, which allowed the car to

be driven flat out for long periods without endangering the life of the engine. It really was possible, even with high-mileage cars, to keep the throttle pedal flat to the boards and cruise at 80mph.

Such treatment certainly made the engine hot and restarting the car after a short break could be a problem, but the owner's manual always recommended that under such circumstances the accelerator pedal should be pushed slowly down when the starter motor was engaged, and for the most part

Karmann's refusal to produce a Type 3 convertible has not prevented fresh air fans from creating their own 'home-built' specials.

this method worked well. Too much or too little throttle and the starter could be spinning seemingly for ever, necessitating a cooling-off period of several minutes, but the simplicity of the flat-four ensured that it would always start in the end.

As an autobahn cruiser the Type 3 was unrivalled in its class, even if its ability to beat the competition from traffic lights was lacking. In comparison, a Lotus Elan could reach 60mph in around 9sec, the same time that it took the Type 3 to reach 40mph. But for VW enthusiasts it did not really matter that their handsome coupé was slow away from the starting blocks. The difference, as always, was that the VW would still be reaching 40mph in 9sec with 150,000 miles on the clock, when its competitors probably would not reach 40mph at all.

In 1963, *Car* magazine carried out an interesting back-to-back test between the Type 3 and the Mk1 Ford Consul Capri. Both had a 1500 engine and both were made to a similar design brief. On performance the Karmann-Ghia proved, surprisingly, to have the edge. The author of the test report commented: 'The VW pulls ahead – literally – in open road give and take thanks to far better torque. It is a pleasure to use in fast traffic where overtaking times are minimal in fourth, with third gear in reserve for really brisk motoring. The Capri scoots right along but it lacks top-gear urge for when you have to step on the floor suddenly.' In conclusion, the report came down heavily against the Capri for its optimistic

speedometer, restless needle and niggling reverse gear lock-out, and favoured the Karmann for its 'high-speed cruising comfort and carefree operation'.

Where handling and roadholding are concerned, the majority of journalists were more impressed with the Type 3 than the Type 1. George Bishop, writing the above-mentioned 'shoot-out' with the Capri for *Car*, actually criticised the Ford's road manners, commenting: 'There is ample poke and the rear wheels spin readily on loose stuff, but equally the tail will slide without much provocation.' These were the sort of views usually aired about Volkswagen's products, but here they were in 1963 being aimed squarely at a Ford.

For enthusiastic drivers who had mastered the Beetle's handling, conducting a Type 3 through a bend at high speed was something of a disappointment because it was so much harder to make the tail break away. The additional weight of the car helped to keep it flatter on the road and, as a result, it was possible to put the power on earlier when exiting a bend. To provoke oversteer the car had to be thrown hard on the steering wheel with the power off and, as soon as the nose was neatly tucked in, it was necessary to bang the throttle pedal down hard, and quickly. With the car off balance, opposite lock could be applied at will and, as long as the power was kept on, a perfect arc would be maintained through the length of a bend.

Those who were sufficiently brave to throw the tail, but who lacked the skill to control the ensuing

The only Karmann-Ghia to be used for an international sporting event was this Type 3, driven by Tony Carter and Sid Davey on the 1965 Monte Carlo Rally. It was in 17th position when an altercation with a snowdrift effectively put it out of contention.

A fully automatic version for 1968 failed to broaden this attractive car's appeal to a wider audience, and in July 1969 the coupé made way for the VW-Porsche 914.

slide by juggling the steering and throttle at the same time, often made the mistake of lifting their foot off the accelerator pedal in mid-corner. At high speeds such foolish action always provoked 'lift-off' oversteer, with the result that the car would spin round in a circle. It was this kind of idiocy among the journalistic fraternity that had got the Beetle an unjustifiable reputation for bad handling, but the Type 3 did not respond readily even to lift-off oversteer. To be perfectly frank, its roadholding in normal driving was a trifle dull, which in 'journalese' means 'safe'.

Incidentally, like the Type 1, the Type 3 was fitted with crossply tyres as standard until the 1969 model year, and they did little to improve roadholding or ride quality. Apart from giving considerably less grip, crossplies wear faster than radials and also have a tendency to follow 'tramlines' in the road irrespective of input from the driver. In fact the only good thing about crossply tyres, as fitted to the Karmann-Ghia, is that they are no longer easy to obtain. Fitting radial tyres today may not find favour with judges of concours d'elegance, but at least the cars that wear modern rubber can be driven a good deal more safely to and from such events.

By contrast, the four-speed Volkswagen all-synchromesh gearbox was never anything less than superb. The ratios were conveniently spaced, with bottom rarely needed for anything other than taking off from rest, and a high ratio on top always made for relaxed cruising. Changes up or down could be achieved as swiftly as it was humanly possible to move the lever, which was most precise in action. And, having been designed to accept engines capable of producing of up to 150bhp, it was one of the car's most durable features.

The worm and roller steering felt good for its day, if woolly by comparison with modern rack-and-pinion systems, but it was light, precise and required 2.8 turns lock to lock. At a diameter of 15.75in, the large steering wheel made for particularly light work at parking speeds even though there was no power assistance. Writing in the Australian magazine *Modern Motor* in 1967, Bryan Hanrahan said: 'You can't get any steering with a better blend of quickness and accuracy than you do in a VW.' And of the brakes he wrote: 'Whatever I did to the Ghia discs I couldn't make them run ragged. The braking with German Dunlops was as good a disc/drum set-up as I've experienced. Pedal pressures were no higher than with the old drum brakes, in spite of no power assistance.'

A 1600 twin-port engine with 90mph potential and a 'luxury' specification for 1968 was 'too little, too late' to save the Type 3 coupé from extinction.

Fuel consumption, which has always been a topic for animated conversation among Volkswagen enthusiasts, was never accurately gauged by contemporary road testers. However, the majority claimed that 28mpg could be expected as an all-round average. In this author's experience between 22-26mpg could be expected by an enthusiastic driver determined to enjoy his or her car, rather than using it to travel from point A to B at the lowest possible speed in top gear, but claims by owners of 35mpg and above can be dismissed as fanciful.

Overall, the Type 3 Karmann-Ghia was a competent, well-built and handsome motor car. It was roomy, reliable and cheap to service. Like all cars, it had its bad points, notably a lack of fresh air ventilation, but that was a small price to pay in a car that could be so rewarding to drive. The quirky styling has always been an acquired taste and the critics were never slow to condemn it. But as the composer, Jean Sibelius, once advised: 'Pay no attention to the critics; no statue has ever been put up to a critic.'

THE KARMANN-GHIA TODAY

It is 20 years since the last Karmann-Ghia Type 1 was made and more than a quarter of a century since the last Type 3 rolled off the Osnabrück assembly lines. Until the late 1970s their numbers fell significantly, rust taking its toll, but the emergence of the classic car movement reversed the decline. Many cars otherwise destined for the scrapheap have been restored to their former glory.

When the classic car boom arrived in the late 1980s and values soared to such artificially high levels, the Karmann-Ghia, and more particularly the Type 1 coupé and convertible, suddenly enjoyed a revival in popularity among Volkswagen enthusiasts, and comparatively large quantities of money exchanged hands for outstanding examples. The Type 1 remains as popular today as ever but, because it was made in such relatively high numbers (more than 440,000

including the convertible), it is unlikely that it will ever become rare. For this reason, it will never command a particularly high price, but for the serious collector there are other problems.

Even in its final 1600 form, the Type 1 never had the performance to accompany its fine looks. Pedestrian acceleration and 50bhp was hardly designed to appeal to the out-and-out sportsman. In short, it went like a Beetle and sounded like one. Although the clattering racket of the air-cooled flat-four is music to the ears of a Volkswagen devotee, it rarely found a sympathetic audience outside the fold. Moreover, the Karmann-Ghia has no motor sport history. No more than a handful were used at club level in minor competitions around the world, and this serious omission from the car's pedigree is sufficient to keep monetary values at a sensible level. However, the

A Type 3 in this condition would test the enthusiasm and patience of the most determined restorer because replacement body panels are almost non-existent.

Type 1 has a particularly large following in the US, Germany, Britain and Australia, even if outside these four countries it remains rare.

For the classic buyer the Karmann-Ghia holds the same attractions as it had for those who bought it new. It can still turn heads and provides an ideal alternative to the Beetle. Because rust was always the car's principal enemy, the best hunting ground today is in California, where the climate is kinder to the handcrafted panelwork than that of Britain or Germany. But beware of advertisements in magazines claiming that a car is 'rust-free', because in recent years it has all too often turned out to be the case that the rust *is* free, and there is plenty of it.

No part of the Type 1's bodywork is immune to corrosion, but particularly vulnerable areas include the wings around the headlamp area, the front and rear wheel arches, the sills, the bottoms of the doors and rear quarter panels, and the front and rear inner wings. The platform chassis has the ability to resist corrosion for many years, but the floorpans on either side of the backbone tunnel can rust through completely.

Because the front and rear wings are welded on to the main body structure, replacing them is not the straightforward job it is on the Beetle, which has bolt-on panels. Repairing a damaged Karmann wing can be a tiresome and expensive business, so parking in confined spaces is best avoided.

Although immensely strong, the front torsion bar tubes are naturally vulnerable, but rust most commonly attacks the 'uprights' which hold them apart, and which carry the mounting points for the shock absorbers. Even quite serious corrosion here is difficult to detect without going to the trouble of jacking up the car and carrying out a detailed inspection with a torch.

The convertible is even more prone to corrosion than the coupé. The hood, although exceptionally tough and well-made, does not last forever, and when the inevitable splits and tears occur even a small amount of water leaking through to the floorpan and sills will eventually take its toll. In addition, the body

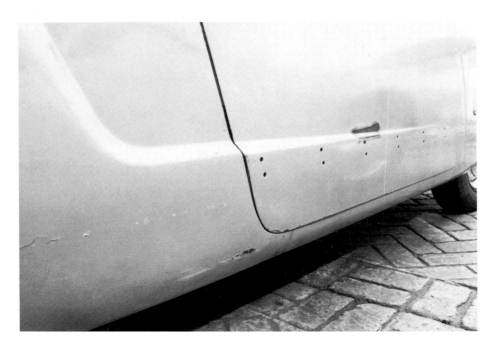

No part of the Karmann's bodyshell is immune to corrosion, and the sills and bottoms of the doors are naturally vulnerable.

flexing that occurs with the convertible imposes heavy loads on the stress-bearing parts of the body strengthening panels, so cracks can open up in the metal on well-used cars. This is rare and only happens with particularly rotten cars, but prospective purchasers should be wary.

Mechanically, air-cooled Volkswagens are among the world's most durable cars, provided they have been maintained and serviced properly. Finding an original car with a full service history these days is a very remote possibility, and in the absence of official documentation, a long test drive and a thorough check of the known weak points will usually reveal any shortcomings.

On high-mileage examples the pushrod tubes notoriously leak oil, but a small amount is perfectly acceptable. It is pointless going to the trouble of stripping down an engine that dribbles out a teaspoon of monograde every 500 miles just to renew the small rubber pushrod seals. Conversely, petrol leaking from the carburettor is usually indicative of a worn throttle spindle – an obvious fire hazard – but replacement carburettors, although expensive, are readily available.

Listening for faults in an engine is not easy, even for an expert. From cold it should feel and sound a little 'lumpy', but a healthy power unit should never take more than two or three minutes to settle down to a smooth idle. A deep growling sound may indicate that the crankshaft bearings are worn, and crankshaft end-float should therefore be checked carefully. The easiest way to do this is to take hold of the crankshaft pulley wheel in both hands and rock it backwards and forwards. If there is any detectable movement, it is safe to assume that the bearings are worn and that the engine is in need of a rebuild. A more accurate check can be carried out with a needle gauge.

In the absence of worn bearings, the most likely source of a growling, rumbling noise is a 'holed' exhaust. Rust most commonly attacks the heat exchangers at the point where they join the tailbox, and even a small hole here can result in the most frightful engine noise. Incidentally, although heat exchangers have been known to last up to 20 years, it is still advisable to replace them regularly. Welding up old heat exchangers usually ends in tears, so it's best not to try. The life of an average tailbox is between two and three years but, unlike the exchangers, replacements are cheap.

On the road, a healthy Karmann-Ghia should feel lively and taut. One that is tired will feel sluggish and sloppy, a possible indication that the cylinder heads are cracked. The later twin-port heads are prone to cracking and, for additional peace of mind, a compression test should be carried out on each cylinder. Pay no attention to those who maintain that the Volkswagen engine is living on borrowed time above 70–80,000 miles. This is a common and oft-heard claim, usually made by people who have a financial interest in providing replacement power units. A car that has been driven sensibly, and had its oil changed and tappet clearances correctly adjusted every 3000 miles, should not require a major overhaul before 150,000 miles. Of course, there are exceptions to every rule…

One particularly common problem is the dreaded dropped valve, which usually occurs on number three cylinder because it is the least well cooled of the four. The usual cause of a dropped valve, and more particularly an exhaust valve, is the prolonged use of high revs over many years. Because the valves are made in two pieces and welded together, excessive heat can cause a weakness in the weld between the stem and the head, and if the latter drops onto the crown of the piston the result is often a catastrophic engine failure.

The steering ought to feel crisp and precise, but with a small amount of free play in the wheel. Similarly, the gearbox should provide an enthusiastic driver with the desire to change up and down more often than is strictly necessary. A lever that jumps out of gear or one that does not slot in smoothly every time may have worn synchromesh or selectors. Less seriously, the rubber mounts under and in front of the 'box may be worn. Rebuilding a worn gearbox is well outside the scope of even the most competent amateur mechanic, but secondhand replacement 'boxes are cheap and plentiful.

The gaiters on the inner ends of the rear axle tubes perish and split in time and allow oil from the gearbox to leak. Naturally, gear wheels do not take kindly to being run without lubrication, but again, a small amount of leakage should not present serious problems as long as the level is topped up.

A juddering or slipping clutch need not give cause for concern because replacements are cheap and easy to fit, but the engine will have to be removed first and there are no short cuts to this operation. Semi-automatic Type 1s are best avoided as they are complex, slow and tend to be fuel thirsty, even if rarity value might increase their attraction for some.

Volkswagen brakes do not give unusual problems as they are entirely conventional. The later cars with dual-circuit systems have a more complicated master cylinder which is more expensive than the earlier single-circuit type, but both types are generally

Today, Karmann-Ghias are as popular as ever and always draw the crowds at Volkswagen shows.

reliable. Seals in the master cylinders will eventually perish and split, meaning that the brake pedal can be pushed down without the car actually stopping, but this does not usually occur without warning signs.

Spare parts for the Type 1 rarely present problems. Because the Beetle is still being produced in Mexico, mechanical components for the 12-volt Karmanns are readily and cheaply available from both the main dealers and independent specialists. The pre-1966 six-volt cars are a little trickier, but good secondhand spares are in plentiful supply. Body panels and hoods for the convertible are also available, mainly through independent suppliers, but tend to be extremely expensive. For the price of a new nosecone, for example, it is still possible to buy a complete Beetle in running order. Some items of trim are now proving difficult to obtain outside Germany, and can also be very expensive.

Collectors tend to favour the 30bhp cars made

A clean, well-maintained engine like this should last for 150,000 miles or more.

between 1955 and 1959 for their rarity value, but it is unlikely that the cost of a professional 'ground-up' restoration could ever be recouped in today's market. Like the vast majority of cars requiring major bodywork and mechanical repairs, the Karmann-Ghia does not make for a sound investment, even in its most desirable and valuable convertible form.

The Type 3 'Razor-edge' is considerably rarer than the Type 1 – only 2500-3000 are thought to exist worldwide – but their sharp decline in numbers over the years has done little to improve their desirability or monetary value. As with the Type 1, the main enemy of the Type 3 is rust, and the heavily salted roads of Europe and Britain have contributed markedly to the wholesale disposal of many from as early as the 1970s.

Naturally, the same principles apply to buying a Type 3 as for the Type 1. They were constructed by the same methods and, by and large, shared the same Wolfsburg mechanical parts bin. Today, restoring one of these fine cars is far from easy. Body panels are virtually unobtainable, and the secondhand ones that turn up from time to time at Volkswagen shows are often expensive and in need of extensive renovation. Exterior and interior pieces of trim seem as extinct as the Dodo. As for the Type 1, mechanical components are easy to obtain, will be in plentiful supply for the

forseeable future and are all reasonably priced whether from main dealers or independent specialists.

The Type 3 is a car for the individualist who wants an 'out of the ordinary' car with all Volkswagen's virtues. There is no doubt that a 'Razor-edge' in good condition provides exceptional value: it offers a lot of car for the money, but persuading a devotee to part with one for mere cash is not usually an easy task. Needless to say, anyone who is offered a Type 3 convertible should remember that genuine production versions were never made, and a home-made job probably is not safe.

Unlike the Type 1, the Type 3 has one claim to sporting fame. Back in 1965 a British dealer, Renwick's of Newton Abbot, entered a 1500 driven by Tony Carter and Sid Davey for the Monte Carlo Rally. The car was specially prepared for this event and its modifications included polished and ported cylinder heads, a special anti-roll bar on the rear suspension, four spotlamps and an additional lamp mounted on the roof, and Dunlop SP3 rally tyres. Unfortunately, the car had an altercation with a large snowdrift close to the finish, but it had been running in 17th position. Carter and Davey eventually completed the course, too late to be officially classified. It is interesting that after the finish of the 1050-mile rally, the SP3 Dunlops showed no detectable signs of wear.

As is the case with all air-cooled Volkswagens, Type 3 running costs are modest, particularly by comparison with other sporting cars from the same period, but one problem that the owners of virtually all classic cars currently share is the likely decline in the availability of leaded fuel. Neither the Type 1 nor the Type 3 were designed to run on unleaded, and anyone faced with an engine rebuild would be wise to consider having the cylinder heads converted. This involves little more than having the valves changed and the valve seats hardened, but the extra expense will surely prove worthwhile.

Ultimately, owning and driving a Type 3 today provides something of a challenge. In view of the shortage of body panels and trim, newcomers to Volkswagens who have set their hearts on one should go for the best car they can afford, preferably one in a roadworthy condition. Attempting to restore a 'basket case' from the ground up will almost certainly disillusion all but the most loyal Volkswagen enthusiast.

THE URGE TO IMPROVE

At the time of the Karmann's launch in 1955 the Beetle had been in production for 10 years, so naturally there were a number of accessories already available for the coupé. Many were aimed at making practical improvements while others provided a means of embellishing and personalising. Some were offered through the official dealer network, but inevitably there were independent manufacturers who had capitalised on the success of the Beetle, and whose parts were available through motor trade distributors.

Typically, most customers specified a Blaupunkt push-button radio, alloy wheel trims and a pair of rear mudflaps – even though the latter never looked right on such a low-slung car. Whitewall tyres were particularly popular in the US and have recently made something of a 'comeback' on both sides of the Atlantic. Porcelain and glass flower vases for mounting on the dashboard were particularly fashionable in the

As popular as ever in the USA, whitewall tyres are also in vogue with Karmann-Ghia owners in Britain and mainland Europe.

late 1950s and 1960s, and although reproductions are available today original items tend to be expensive.

Additional instruments included a fuel gauge that fitted next to the speedometer. Alternatively, there was a more comprehensive instrument cluster, mounted on a chromed panel, that included a fuel gauge, a clock and an oil pressure gauge. Designed to fit in the middle of the dash panel in place of a radio, this cluster was more suited to the Beetle, because Karmann owners who availed themselves of it acquired a second clock…

Particularly useful early accessories were a hand-operated extension handle for the reserve petrol tap, a puller for removing the hubcaps, and an anti-theft

A fake radiator grille found favour in some quarters! This Malta-registered car is also peculiar in having a pre-1959 left-hand wing and a post-1959 right-hand one.

device that fitted at the bottom of the gear stick, locking it into place. The chromed grilles that fit over the air intake louvres, while popular, have a tendency to trap moisture and cause corrosion.

One of the most sought-after accessories is a tool kit, which sits within the spare wheel. Apart from containing some useful tools, the kit comes in a round metal casing stamped with the V-over-W emblem and looks most attractive. A heavily-dished three-spoke 'sports' steering wheel was also available in the late 1950s and early 1960s, but as it had a rather ugly full-circle horn ring and relied heavily on chromium-plating for the spokes, it is not easy to understand where its sporting appeal lay.

The lists of 'optional extras' available in the showrooms differed widely from country to country, and depended very much on the rules and regulations governing each particular export market. For example, British and American exports obviously had speedometers calibrated in miles, rather than kilometres, per hour, and until the end of July 1966 customers in Australia and Italy could choose to have yellow tail lights.

From the beginning of the 1966 model year, export cars came with the option of a 'Volkswagen' script on the engine lid instead of one that read 'VW 1300' (or 'VW 1500' the following year). For the US and Canada, there were sealed beam headlamps, red tail lights, flashing indicators with side marker lamps, a

dual-circuit brake warning light and parking lamps. For the following year the same list included a buzzer for the ignition starter switch. Cars destined for the pollution- and safety-conscious Californian market were fitted with an activated carbon container for absorbing fuel vapour (now a standard fitment on Mexican Beetles) for the 1970 model year.

Tuning and customising ....

Accessories and extras inevitably played an important role in the lives of everyday Karmann-Ghia people, but for real excitement enthusiastic drivers turned towards the tuning and performance market. There were no 'bolt-on', 'go-faster' goodies available from Volkswagen, which took the view that 'speed merchants' should go to Stuttgart to satisfy their desire for an excess of adrenalin, so it was left to the independent specialists to provide the necessary bits and pieces to make the performance of a Karmann match its looks.

During the early days, the easiest way to make a Karmann-Ghia faster was to fit a Porsche 356 engine and gearbox, but that was well beyond the reach of the majority of Volkswagen's clientele. Fortunately, help was at hand. The German company, Okrasa (now Oettinger), started offering engine tuning kits for Beetles in the early 1950s and, not surprisingly, the idea soon caught on with Karmann owners.

THE URGE TO IMPROVE

Helmut Meidt's 1600 Karmann is also fitted with a fake radiator grille, but to a different design.

The 'sports' steering wheel that became available in the early 1960s is now very rare, but the passage of 30 years has done little to increase its desirability.

The Okrasa kit, which boosted the power output of the 30bhp engine by about 30 per cent, consisted of a pair of Solex 32mm carburettors and twin-port cylinder heads (for improved breathing) machined to increase the compression ratio to 7.5:1. Further tuning components were introduced on the 34bhp engine, including larger pistons and barrels to give a displacement of 1300cc and a heavy-duty long-stroke crankshaft with a 69.5mm stroke. In the latter guise, the car's top speed went up to around 90–95mph and the 0–60mph time came down to around 14sec.

Another German company, Denzel, made a number of tuning 'goodies' (including twin-port cylinder heads) and in Britain the Speedwell company (of which the late Graham Hill was a director) marketed all sorts of bolt-ons, including a rear

'stabiliser' bar that went a long way towards negating the 'jacking up' effect of the swing-axle suspension under hard cornering. In America Gene Berg reworked his own Volkswagen engine for better performance and, along with Joe Vittone and Dean Lowry of the original EMPI company, started a VW tuning industry that in the 1990s is bigger than ever.

During the 1960s, superchargers enjoyed a minor revival, the Judson becoming a firm favourite with Volkswagen owners. But there were others, including the Shorrocks, MAG and Fageol 'Pepco'. They all worked well, even if it was sometimes at the expense of increased fuel consumption. Fitting a supercharger to a 1200 engine gave similar performance to the later standard 1600 engines, but a 'blower' in good condition is now considered highly collectable. There are also much easier and cheaper ways of extracting more power from the flat-four.

In recent years considerable efforts have been made, particularly in America, to develop the air-cooled Volkswagen engine. The results are simply astonishing. A number of specialist companies have reworked virtually every one of the Volkswagen's mechanical components for greater strength and power, to the point where figures of 300bhp and more are commonplace.

During the mid-1960s the inspiration for such power was provided by the American drag racing scene. The superior traction afforded by the

Dechromed bodywork, lowered suspension and a bright paint job are all hallmarks of the popular Cal-look (right). Haberdashery stores can provide limitless inspiration for fabric covers (below right)...

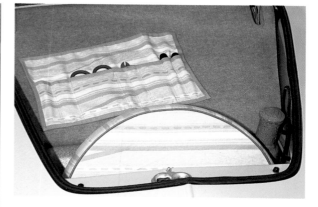

Hip-hugging leather seats and a large tachometer add individualism and style to this 'Looker'.

A brace of twin-choke Webers, a Bosch 009 distributor and a Monza 'four-prong' exhaust system.

Larger barrels and pistons, twin carburettors and a host of tuning 'goodies' are available from independent Volkswagen specialists.

Volkswagen, with the weight of its engine and gearbox concentrated over the rear wheels, makes for fast acceleration from a standing start on the quarter-mile drag strips. As the tuning industry progressed with its development, Volkswagens began to take the place of the V8 Chevies and Fords as the cars to beat. Today, air-cooled Volkswagens are among the fastest quarter-milers in the world, but the special equipment necessary for producing a sub 10sec run is, needless to say, very expensive.

While Volkswagen drag racing was getting off the ground in America, the first 'Cal-look' cars also emerged from West Coast tuning shops, starting a fashion that by the mid-1980s had spread to Britain and the rest of Europe. A customising style that emulates the 'dumped-on-the-ground' drag cars, Cal-look is aimed at improving the Karmann-Ghia (and other air-cooled Volkswagens) in appearance and performance. Typically, the bodywork is relieved of its bumpers and superfluous trim and repainted in a bright colour, the suspension is lowered front and rear, and the standard wheels are substituted for a set of alloys.

In addition, the interior is retrimmed to suit individual taste, often to Porsche standards, and the engine is reworked for additional power. The essence of the Cal-look theme is to enhance the original Volkswagen design by simplifying it. With the exterior trim removed, the shape of the bodywork can be more readily appreciated – or so the theory goes – and with considerably more horses under the rear lid than

A Judson supercharger is one way of boosting the power output, but there are easier ways of tuning the VW engine today.

Volkswagen originally intended, driving a Cal-looker for many devotees becomes the ultimate motoring pleasure.

Shifting into Top Ghia..........................

Because the Volkswagen engine was designed to be durable and reliable, its ability to rev and produce useable performance has been intentionally restricted. The small Solex carburettor, narrow inlet ports and

Lowered suspension and Porsche alloy wheels give this Karmann-Ghia convertible a more purposeful look.

docile camshaft all conspire to offer the enthusiastic driver a leisurely and uninspiring motoring career, but, largely thanks to the Americans, there is much one can do to improve the Karmann-Ghia's performance without even removing the engine.

The 50bhp 1600 twin-port engine naturally lends itself to tuning more readily than the smaller capacity single-port engines, and power output can be greatly improved by making a few simple changes. The first thing to do is to remove the standard exhaust system and replace it with one of the dozens of specially tuned systems available from independent specialists. It is important to select one that incorporates pipes of equal length between the cylinder heads and the tailbox, so that exhaust gases are allowed to escape at equal pressure.

This step alone will only give a small increase in power, perhaps just 2bhp, so the next stage is to replace the standard carburettor with a progressive twin-choke Weber. The advantage of this is that only one choke opens at a time, so it is possible to save fuel at low cruising speeds. When additional performance is required, the second choke opens in response to a wider throttle opening.

A Bosch 009 all-centrifugal distributor will improve the ignition advance system, but should be timed with a strobe to 28 degrees of advance at 3000rpm. High-ratio rockers and performance pushrods can also be installed without removing the engine and, because they open up the valves further than the standard items, allow a greater quantity of the fuel/air mixture into the combustion chambers. One other small 'tweak' is to exchange the standard crankshaft pulley for a small-diameter item and fit a shorter fan belt. This modification reduces the drag created by the engine's cooling fan, but because it also reduces its cooling efficiency it is not always a good idea in warm climates.

All of the above modifications will give a 'sensible' increase in performance – around 10-15bhp – without

Porsche instruments are no easier to see through a 911 steering wheel when they are fitted to a Karmann, but what style!

compromising reliability, but to experience the delights (and drawbacks) of high performance, it is necessary to remove the engine from the car and strip it down. At this stage, check the condition of the crankcase and particularly the bearing saddles, crankshaft, conrods and flywheel, all of which receive a hammering on abused or high-mileage engines. Common problems which can develop with the VW engine include hairline cracks in the crankshaft, scoring or evidence of buffeting on the saddles as a result of worn bearings, and cracks in the face of the crankcase behind the flywheel.

Obviously, it may be possible to get away with line-boring a worn crankcase, but where there are cracks the case will have to be scrapped and a replacement found. Having established that these basic components are in good condition, the next stage is to decide on the required specification and the car's eventual application. It is possible these days to build a 3-litre engine with nitrous oxide injection, a turbocharger and a 'wild' camshaft that will take a Karmann from rest to 100mph in less than 5sec, but there is not much point in pursuing this route if the aim is for a little harmless fun on a Sunday afternoon's cruise into the countryside.

For road use it is preferable to keep everything within sensible limits for the sake of retaining the car's driveability. Fitting larger barrels and pistons is the

most obvious way of producing more power, and there are various sizes available. Engine capacities of 1641cc, 1679cc, 1776cc and 1835cc are the most popular but, for the latter two, the standard crankcase and heads will have to be machined to allow the larger barrels to fit. Larger capacity barrels are available, including 2, 2.1, 2.2, 2.4 and 3 litres, but are not generally suitable for road applications.

The standard camshaft has very little worth in a tuned engine but the American-made Engle 110 is a useful alternative. Work to the standard cylinder heads should normally involve removing burrs or other imperfections in the metal around the ports, matching the ports for an exact fit to the manifold and exhaust, replacing the valve guides, and fitting new valves and heavy-duty springs.

Other modifications include trimming the flywheel down to a weight of around 13lb, balancing the conrods and pistons so that they are equal in weight, and fitting an external oil cooler and an oil sump extension. To ensure that the engine is fed properly, a brace of 40IDF Weber or 40DRLA Dell'Orto carburettors with the appropriate linkages are the most popular choice, and work well.

It is possible to go much further up the tuning

A set of ATS five-spoke alloys improves the sporting appearance of this Type 3.

Lowering the suspension can enhance the Karmann-Ghia's roadholding, but with a standard 1600 engine the top speed of this convertible is roughly the same as that of the bus behind it.

Stylish five-spoke Empis are inexpensive alternatives to the Porsche wheels. Note that the wings have been modified to suit the headlamp cowls.

ladder, and exactly where one stops is usually governed by how much one wants to spend. It is beyond the scope of this book to go into detail about such devices as counterweighted stroker crankshafts, but suffice to say that it is difficult to go far wrong by sticking to the tried and tested tuning methods.

The idea of tuning air-cooled Volkswagens for greater performance started in the 1950s and shows no signs of abating in the 1990s. Such is the enthusiasm for VWs that a thriving multi-million pound industry has grown up with the Karmann and the Beetle.

Thanks to this industry it is now possible to carry out a whole host of modifications to improve these cars, which form the centrepiece of so many motoring lives. Today, a number of off-the-shelf devices are available for lowering the torsion bar suspension, and there are special racing gearboxes, massive ranges of special wheels and tyres, engine dress-up kits and glass-fibre body panels.

In the 1990s the future of the Karmann-Ghia looks brighter than at any time in the past. Long live the Karmann-Ghia.

APPENDIX

When referring to Karmann-Ghias, Volkswagen type numbers relate to the chassis and not to the body styles mounted on them. The air-cooled Volkswagen types are as follows: Beetle, Type 1; Transporter, Type 2; Notchback saloon, variant (estate version) and fastback, Type 3; 411 and 412, Type 4. The Type 1 Karmann-Ghia is based on the Beetle platform chassis and the Type 3 Karmann-Ghia is based on the variant's platform chassis. Because the Osnabrück company did not make a production car based on either the Transporter or Type 4 chassis, there was never a Type 2 or Type 4 Karmann-Ghia.

For identification purposes in Volkswagen's parts lists, both Karmann-Ghia type numbers are followed by the number 4 to distinguish them from Beetles and Type 3s, and then by another number to distinguish the Karmann models from each other.

The numbers relating to Karmann-Ghias are as follows:

LHD Type 1 convertible	141
RHD Type 1 convertible	142
LHD Type 1 coupé	143
RHD Type 1 coupé	144
LHD Type 3 coupé	343
RHD Type 3 coupé	344
LHD Type 3 coupé with electric sunroof	345
RHD Type 3 coupé with electric sunroof	346

Colours......................................

MODEL 143/144
To Aug 1957
Black, Deep Green, Trout Blue, Gazelle-Beige, Deep Brown
Sep 1957 to Jul 1959
Black, Bamboo, Aero Silver, Dolphin Blue, Cognac, Brilliant Red, Cardinal Red
Aug 1959 to Jul 1960
Black, Mango Green, Seagull Grey, Midnight Blue, Strato Blue, Malachite Green, Paprika

MODEL 141/142
To Dec 1958
Black, Pearl White, Diamond Grey, Cardinal Red, Amazon, Graphite Silver, Bernina

Jan 1959 to Jul 1959
Black, Pearl White, Diamond Grey, Cardinal Red, Amazon, Graphite Silver, Bernina
Aug 1959 to Jul 1960
Black, Pearl White, Platinum Grey, Sea Blue, Malachite Green, Paprika, Ferrite Brown

MODEL 141-144
Aug 1960 to Jul 1962
Black, Pearl White, Sea Blue, Pampas Green, Lavender, Pacific, Paprika Red, Ruby Red, Anthracite, Sierra Beige
Aug 1962 to Jul 1963
Black, Pearl White, Sea Blue, Pacific, Ruby Red, Anthracite, Emerald, Polar Blue, Manila Yellow, Terra Brown
Aug 1963 to Jul 1964
Black, Pearl White, Sea Blue, Pacific, Ruby Red, Anthracite, Emerald Green, Polar Blue, Manila Yellow, Terra Brown
Aug 1964 to Jul 1965
Bermuda, Sea Blue, Roulette Green, Henna Red, Cherry Red, Manila Yellow, Sea Sand, Arcona White, Smoke Grey, Fontana Grey, Black
Aug 1965 to Jul 1966
Black, Bermuda, Sea Blue, Roulette Green, Henna Red,

An early colour chart from 1958.

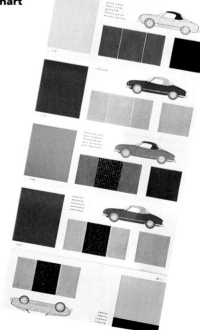

Cherry Red, Manila Yellow, Sea Sand, Arcona White (to Jan 1966, chassis number 146 531 868), Lotus White (from Feb 1966, chassis number 146 531 869)

Aug 1966 to Jul 1967
Black, Bermuda, Lotus White, Roulette Green, Cherry Red, Savanna Beige, Castilian Yellow, Neptune Blue, Vulkan Grey

Aug 1967 to Jul 1968
Velour Red, Black, Regatta Blue, Pine Green, Chinchilla, Gobi Beige, Lotus White, Bermuda, Cherry Red

Aug 1968 to Jul 1969
Oriole Yellow, Sunset, Chrome Blue, Cypress Green, Toga White, Cherry Red

Aug 1969 to Jul 1970
Pampas Yellow, Amber, Bahia Red, Black, Albery Blue, Pastel Blue, Irish Green, Light Ivory

Aug 1970 to Jul 1971
Bahia Red, Black, Adria Blue, Irish Green, Willow Green, Light Ivory, Amber, Blood Orange, Silver Metallic, Gemini Metallic, Gold Metallic, Lemon Yellow

Aug 1971 to Jul 1972
Bahia Red, Black, Adria Blue, Irish Green, Willow Green, Light Ivory, Amber, Blood Orange, Silver Metallic, Gemini Metallic, Gold Metallic, Saturn Yellow

From Aug 1972
Black, Light Ivory, Bahia Red, Amber, Saturn Yellow, Olympic Blue, Phoenix Red, Sunshine Yellow, Zambesi Green, Ravenna Green, Saturn Yellow Metallic, Alaska Metallic, Marathon Metallic

MODEL 343/344/345/346
To Jul 1962
Black, Pearl White, Ruby Red, Anthracite, Sea Blue, Pacific

Aug 1962 to Jul 1964
Black, Ruby Red, Sea Blue, Pearl White, Anthracite, Polar Blue, Terra Brown, Manila Yellow, Emerald, Pacific

Aug 1964 to Jul 1965
Bermuda, Smoke Grey, Cherry Red, Henna Red, Roulette Green, Arcona White, Fontana Grey, Sea Blue, Manila Yellow, Sea Sand

Aug 1965 to Jul 1966
Bermuda, Cherry Red, Henna Red, Roulette Green, Arcona White (to Jan 1966, chassis number 346 147 892), Lotus White (from Feb 1966, chassis number 346 147 893), Black, Sea Blue, Manila Yellow, Sea Sand

Aug 1966 to Jul 1967
Bermuda, Savanna Beige, Vulkan Grey, Cherry Red, Neptune Blue, Castilian Yellow, Roulette Green, Lotus White, Black

Aug 1967 to Jul 1968
Velour Red, Black, Regatta Blue, Pine Green, Chinchilla, Gobi Beige, Lotus White, Bermuda, Cherry Red

Aug 1968 to Jul 1969
Oriole Yellow, Sunset, Chrome Blue, Cypress Green, Toga White, Cherry Red

Chassis numbers

TYPE 1

Aug 1955[1]	929 746
Dec 1955	1 060 929
Dec 1956	1 394 119
Aug 1957[2]	1 600 440
Sep 1957	1 649 253
Dec 1957	1 774 680
Dec 1958	2 226 206
Aug 1959[3]	2 528 668
Dec 1959	2 801 613
Aug 1960	3 192 507
Dec 1960	3 551 044
Aug 1961	4 010 995
Dec 1961	4 400 051
Aug 1962	4 846 836
Dec 1962	5 199 980
Aug 1963	5 677 119
Dec 1963	6 016 120
Aug 1964	145 000 001
Dec 1964	145 396 732
Aug 1965	146 000 001
Dec 1965	146 463 103
Aug 1966	147 000 001
Dec 1966	147 442 503
Aug 1967	148 000 001
Dec 1967	148 398 736
Aug 1968	149 000 001
Dec 1968	149 474 780
Aug 1969	140 2000 001
Dec 1969	140 2402 623
Aug 1970	141 2000 001
Dec 1970	141 2435 197
Aug 1971	142 2000 001
Feb 1972	142 2432 709
Aug 1972	143 2000 001
Aug 1973	144 2000 001

Note
Except where clarified by a footnote, chassis numbers are the last built in each month.

[1] Type 143 introduced
[2] Type 141 introduced
[3] Types 142 and 144 introduced

TYPE 3

Sep 1961[1]	00 269
Dec 1961	10 550
Jul 1962[2]	50 282
Aug 1962	64 916
Dec 1962	138 774
Aug 1963	221 975
Dec 1963	321 076
Aug 1963	221 975
Dec 1963	321 076
Jan 1964[3]	341 651
Feb 1964[4]	342 081
Aug 1964	345 000 001
Dec 1964	345 087 857
Aug 1965	346 000 001
Dec 1965	346 140 226
Aug 1966	347 000 001
Dec 1966	347 134 254
Aug 1967	348 000 001
Dec 1967	348 079 424
Aug 1968	349 000 001
Dec 1968	349 108 899
Jul 1969	349 500 000

Note
Except where clarified by a footnote, chassis numbers are the last built in each month.

[1] Type 343 introduced
[2] Type 345 introduced
[3] Type 344 introduced
[4] Type 346 introduced

Production figures...........................

TYPE 1 COUPE

Year	Units	Year	Units
1955	1,282	1961	3,965
1956	11,555	1962	4,570
1957	15,369	1963	5,433
1958	14,515	1964	5,262
1959	17,196	1965	5,326
1960	19,259	1966	5,395
1961	16,708	1967	4,183
1962	18,812	1968	5,713
1963	22,829	1969	6,504
1964	25,267	1970	6,398
1965	28,387	1971	6,565
1966	23,387	1972	2,910
1967	19,406	1973	2,555
1968	24,729		
1969	27,834	**Total**	**80,899**
1970	24,893		
1971	21,133		
1972	12,434	**TYPE 3 COUPE**	
1973	10,462	1961	661
1974	7,167	1962	8,541
		1963	6,720
Total	**363,401**	1964	7,367
		1965	6,873
		1966	5,947
		1967	2,819
CONVERTIBLE		1968	2,533
1957	105	1969	1,049
1958	4,392		
1959	4,585	**Total**	**42,498**
1960	5,465		

Technical specifications.........................

TYPE 1 KARMANN-GHIA (1955)

Engine Horizontally-opposed air-cooled four-cylinder **Construction** Alloy crankcase made in two halves split vertically down the middle and bolted together; heavily-finned cylinder barrels made of cast iron, alloy cylinder heads **Main bearings** Four **Bore × stroke** 77mm × 64mm **Capacity** 1192cc (72.7cu in) **Valves** Pushrod ohv **Compression ratio** 6.6:1 **Fuel system** Bosch mechanical fuel pump, single Solex 28 PCI carburettor **Maximum power** 30bhp at 3400rpm **Maximum torque** 64lb ft at 2400rpm **Transmission** Four-speed gearbox without synchromesh on bottom. Gear ratios: first, 3.60; second 1.88; third, 1.23; fourth, 0.82; reverse, 4.53; final drive, 4.43:1. 180mm clutch **Brakes** Hydraulic Ate-Simplex 9in drums all round **Front suspension** Transverse torsion bars, twin trailing arms, double-acting telescopic shock absorbers, anti-roll bar **Rear suspension** Transverse torsion bars, trailing arms, swing axles, double-acting telescopic shock absorbers **Steering** Worm and nut steering gearbox with 2.4 turns lock to lock **Dry weight** 1742lb (790kg) **Kerb weight** 2448lb (1110kg) **Wheels & tyres** 4J×15in pressed steel wheels, 5.60×15 cross-ply tyres **Top speed** 76mph **0–60mph** 28sec **Max speed in gears** First, 20mph; second, 38mph; third, 63mph **Top gear per 1000rpm** 20.2mph **Length** 163in (4140mm) **Width** 64.2in (1630mm) **Height** 52.2in (1325mm) **Wheelbase** 94.5in (2400mm)

TYPE 3 KARMANN-GHIA (1961)

As Type 1 except: **Construction** Cooling fan mounted at rear of engine instead of vertically above it **Bore × stroke** 83mm × 69mm **Capacity** 1493cc (91.1cu in) **Compression ratio** 7.8:1 **Fuel system** Bosch mechanical fuel pump, single Solex 32 PHN-1 carburettor **Maximum power** 45bhp at 3800rpm **Maximum torque** 78lb ft at 2000rpm **Transmission** Four-speed gearbox with synchromesh on all forward speeds. Gear ratios: first, 3.80; second 2.06; third, 1.32; fourth, 0.89; reverse, 3.88; final drive, 4.125:1. 200mm clutch **Brakes** Hydraulic 9.8in drums all round **Dry weight** 2006lb (910kg) **Kerb weight** 2889lb (1310kg) **Wheels & tyres** 4J×15in pressed steel wheels, 6.00×15 cross-ply tyres **Top speed** 82mph **0–60mph** 21sec **Max speed in gears** First, 30mph; second, 49mph; third, 68mph **Top gear per 1000rpm** 19.8mph **Length** 168.5in (4280mm) **Width** 63.8in (1620mm) **Height** 52.6in (1335mm) **Wheelbase** 94.5in (2400mm)

Cruising along the banks of the River Seine in Paris, the perfect place for christening a convertible after a long, arduous restoration.

ACKNOWLEDGEMENTS

The author is grateful for the immense help offered by the Karmann-Ghia Owners Club of Great Britain, particularly by Derek Frow, during the preparation of this book. The cars photographed by Paul Debois specifically for this book are owned by Derek Frow, Darin Frow, John Figg and Andy Holmes. Combe Grove Manor Hotel and Prior Park College, both in Bath, kindly allowed their grounds to be used for photography. Other photographs were supplied by Derek Frow (that man again!), Yan Rami, Laurence Meredith and Marco Batazzi. Sources of historic photographs were Karmann GMbH, Andy Holmes, David Hodges and Otis Meyer of *Road & Track* magazine.